Contents

Acknowledgments

Greg Swartz thanks Jim Bramsen, Joseph Bruno, Mike D'Onofrio, Dave Foy, Dave Forrester, Doug Hawken, Frankie Ho, Kevin Point, Jeff Settano, John K. Solheim, John Solheim, Brian Weeks, and Andrew Wert. He especially thanks Natalie, Ireland, and Nicholas.

Julie Thorpe thanks Ashley Andrew, Susan Dunlap, Stella Elting, Mary Collins Frank, April Fugle, Beth Hartauer, Cindy Humm, Steve Kling, Judy Kuhn, Julie Long, Jack Mandru, Barbara Meyer, Marcia Moses, Carol Nealley, Candice Somers, Earl Strong, Conna Tigges, John Swartz, and Kay Swartz. She especially thanks Brendan, Dylan, Kylie, and Ralph Thorpe.

Finally, both Julie and Greg thank you for reading this book and invite your feedback; please get in touch with them at www.leadershiplessonsbook.com or at greg@leadership lessonsbook.com and julie@leadershiplessonsbook.com.

A Note About the Origins of This Book

This book is a modified version of the popular book *Seeing David in the Stone* (published in 2006 by Leading Books Press and authored by James B. Swartz and Joseph E. Swartz with contributions by Greg Swartz, Julie K. Thorpe, and John Swartz). The original book was an interesting travelogue reported through the voice of a fictional character named Mike Thoms, president of Dardenn Corporation. Readers of this original version are invited to listen in on the conversations between Mike and a researcher named Marcus as they travel around Europe and other locations sipping expresso in the plazas and cafés and discussing the leadership qualities of Michelangelo, Einstein, Bill Gates, and other well-known individuals. *Leadership Lessons* can be considered a more traditional business version of this original work.

Prologue

Throughout history, people have debated about why some achieve much greater success than others. These are the four most widely believed theories:

- Hard work, perseverance, risk taking, and superior individual habits are the essentials for great success.
- Everyone is capable of great success. You just have to find a way to get beyond your fears to discover and liberate the creativity within you.
- Big breaks come from being in the right place, with the right people, at the right time.
- Heredity and early environment form the basis for future success.

The Truth and Limits of Success Theories

There is truth in each of these theories of why people succeed. But the last two suggest that there is a "life lottery" determining your chances of success. The life lottery idea is comforting for those who have accomplished little. It's hopeful for those who believe in luck. It's disheartening for those who believe they were not given a great start in life. It's a good excuse for doing little to prepare for success. And it does not inspire us to greatness.

The most successful people do not live their lives as if they believed in a life lottery. They believe that you can create your own future. And because they believe this, they search for and discover a path that can lead to great success.

The first two theories acknowledge that the individual has some control over his or her success, but they fall short of explaining the achievements of most of the highly successful people who were studied in researching this book.

Consider Leonardo da Vinci. The historian Vasari called him superhuman. Leonardo da Vinci was an illegitimate child of a notary and a peasant girl, and thus by tradition he could only enter a working-class trade. Drafting, art, and science were considered working-class trades at that time, so when he showed some early signs of liking to draw, he was encouraged by his father. In 1466, at the age of 14 years, he was apprenticed as a studio boy in an art *bottega* owned by Andrea del Verrocchio, a leading painter and sculptor. From this humble beginning, he went on to produce the *Mona Lisa*, *The Last Supper*, a vast treasure of engineering drawings of his inventions, and extensive writings full of powerful insights.

There are people who say that Bill Gates benefited from the third theory—that he was in the right place at the right time. But they don't know the whole story. His lucky break supposedly came 25 years ago when his friend Paul Allen walked by a newsstand in Harvard Square. A photo on the front cover of a magazine caught Allen's eye. The headline above the picture said, "Breakthrough—World's First Minicomputer." Allen grabbed a copy and ran across campus to tell Gates that the revolution had started without them. The next morning, Gates and Allen called Altair, the company that built the tiny computer, and claimed that they had a software program that would run on it. Then, in a two-week burst of creativity, they wrote a software program that actually did what they had claimed.

Many leaders of major computer companies also saw that article and dismissed the tiny computer as a plaything. But Gates and Allen saw the potential. They knew they had the software expertise and that, if they moved fast, they could seize the opportunity. The company they built, Microsoft, today is the largest personal computer software company in the world, and both men have earned vast fortunes. So why didn't other software experts and leaders of large computer companies see the opportunity? Weren't they also in the right place at the right time with the right people?

Strategic Keys to Success

We believe that none of the most popular theories adequately explains the success of da Vinci and Gates. Instead, their success came from following the same path to greatness as followed by Winston Churchill, Marie Curie, Thomas Edison, Albert Einstein, Dwight D. Eisenhower, Galileo Galilei, Abraham Lincoln, Fred Smith, Sam Walton, Oprah Winfrey, and Frank Lloyd Wright, to name a few. In this book, these and others are called the "great achievers."

In more than 20 years of research, we have discovered that all these great achievers have followed a path guided by 10 powerful strategic keys to the overall strategy of pursuing opportunities, mobilizing support, and seizing opportunities. These keys—rather than heredity, traits, intelligence, environment, or work habits—have made

the great achievers more successful than others. In recent years, we have been helping individuals and organizations to grow and prosper using the keys. We have
shown how anyone, at any age, can use them to succeed.

These 10 strategic keys to success are needed today more than ever. For example, in
the past 10 years, Asia's industrial might and innovative capabilities have risen rapidly. Asian firms can produce a lower-cost version of most products and a lower-cost
alternative to many services, and they can do high-quality research and software
development at a fraction of the cost of the same work done in the United States,
Canada, and Europe. In the competitive global economy, the ability to realize the
highest potential achievement has become a critical competence for the survival for
both individuals and organizations. The 10 keys can bring greatness to your own life
and help you lead others to greatness.

Part I

Pursue High-Leverage Opportunities

Now, a few words on looking for things. When you go looking for something specific, your chances of finding it are very bad. Because of all the things in the world, you're only looking for one of them. When you go looking for anything at all, your chances of finding it are very good. Because of all the things in the world, you're sure to find some of them.

—Daryl Zero, *The Zero Effect*

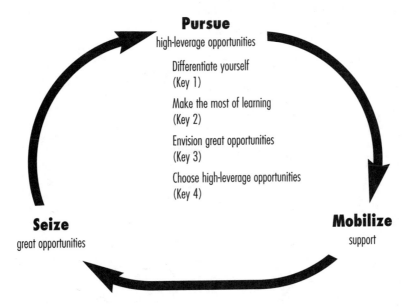

Pursue
high-leverage opportunities

Differentiate yourself
(Key 1)

Make the most of learning
(Key 2)

Envision great opportunities
(Key 3)

Choose high-leverage opportunities
(Key 4)

Seize
great opportunities

Mobilize
support

A high-leverage opportunity is a prospective situation whose value is much higher than the amount of energy or resources needed to seize it. That is, when presented with a set of opportunities, the ones that have highest value and require the lowest expenditure of resources to successfully capture are the high-leverage opportunities. The diagram on the previous page illustrates the iterative process of pursuing opportunities, mobilizing support, and seizing opportunities. The great achievers pursue this finding-and-seizing process again and again to dominate their domain. Part I of this book explains keys 1 through 4 to pursuing this process, as shown in the diagram.

It is often said that you should learn everything that you can, because it will determine your level of success. But the world's greatest achievers have used different strategies to learn. They have concentrated their learning in areas where they have passion, advantage, and rewards. They have used techniques to find and efficiently process knowledge. They have used methods to cut to the core of what is most important to their field. They have been able to envision opportunities and maximize their achievement by concentrating only on those with the greatest chance of making them successful. And thus they have embodied the 10 keys. Their insights and methods for pursuing high-leverage opportunities are presented in keys 1 through 4.

The first great achiever we describe was a legendary genius. He is an excellent example of the importance of key 1—the gateway key—to the success of the great achievers.

Key 1

Differentiate Yourself

It is not enough to have a good mind. The main thing is to use it well.

—René Descartes

For years, a German clerk worked by day at a patent office in Zurich as a patent reviewer because no one would give him a job in physics, his chosen field. After work, he returned to his drafty, one-room apartment in Zurich to spend his evenings studying the mysteries of time and motion. In 1905, this unknown clerk published papers on Brownian motion, the photoelectric effect, and the Theory of Relativity. The paper on the photoelectric effect eventually won him a Nobel Prize. The paper titled "The Special Theory of Relativity" changed the face of physics forever.

This clerk, Albert Einstein, suffered from dyslexia and, up to the age of seven, had difficulty speaking, having to repeat words to himself slowly. As a child, he was mentally slow and failed mathematics in his early school years. His teacher advised his father that he needn't concern himself with choosing a line of work for his son, because the boy wouldn't amount to anything. Until his research papers catapulted him to international fame, he was an outsider and ignored by his peers in science (figure 1-1).

By the age of 20, Einstein had obtained a degree in physics from the Swiss Polytechnic School, with a B average. His professors gave him poor evaluations, saying that he was rebellious and skipped classes. With poor evaluations, he couldn't get a teaching post or a job in physics, so he took the job as a clerk.

Figure 1-1. Albert Einstein, 1905 (© ImageState)

The research team for this book struggled with Einstein. Some said that lessons learned from geniuses don't apply to the average person. Then one researcher asked, "If Einstein had chosen to be a great patent reviewer, would we consider him a genius today?" The other researchers agreed that the answer was "no," because Einstein had no passion for patent review, he was not exceptional at it, there was no opportunity in it to do something revolutionary, and he had little chance of great rewards. His passion, talent, and potential rewards were in physics, and that's where he searched for opportunity.

The Gateway Key to Success

The "great achievers"—the great leaders who are the source of the 10 keys—knew where to focus their life work to achieve success. They focused on three basic factors:

- where they had passion for their work
- what they did far better than others
- where there were potential rewards for their work.

The great achievers thus chose to work where their passions, their abilities, and their potential rewards were all high. For example, the young Thomas Edison chose to be a telegraph operator because he loved it, was good at it, and the telegraph was the Internet of his time.

But what about Leonardo da Vinci? If he had been allowed to follow the field of his ancestors and became a notary, would we consider him superhuman? We suspect he would have become a great notary and businessman, and he would have been admired and respected in his times. However, it's hard to imagine that we would think of him as superhuman today.

Finding Where to Search Late in Life

Some people spend years searching for opportunity where the rewards will never be there for them. But the great achievers never stop searching. Colonel Harland Sanders is a good example. All his life, he moved from sales job to sales job, living from paycheck to paycheck. At the age of 65, he finally found his opportunity when he moved to Corbin, Kentucky, to run a gas station. To increase sales at the station, he started serving fried chicken made from his special recipe. Business boomed.

Then a new interstate highway bypassed Corbin, and the business failed. Devastated, Sanders assessed his life. He decided that he knew how to fry chicken better than anyone else, loved to cook, and loved to sell. So he traveled around the country calling on restaurants. He would cook a batch of chicken for each owner, and then sell a franchise. By the age of 75, he had more than 600 franchisees. He never settled until he found a way to differentiate himself from the crowd and, when he did, he found great opportunity.

Organizations Change How They Are Differentiated

The noted researcher Jim Collins found that great organizations can also change late in life if they realize that they no longer can be the best at what they do. He uses the example of Abbott Laboratories, which knew in 1964 that its competitors like Merck had powerful laboratories that made them the best in the world at creating drugs.

Although Abbott's core competence and principal source of revenue was drug production, its leaders knew that it couldn't continue to be the best in this field in the long run. So they searched for what Abbott could do best. They decided to create products that make health care more cost-effective, products that help a patient regain strength quickly after surgery, and diagnostics that improve a physician's ability to find the correct causes. Today, Abbott continues to be successful in the health care field. For more, see Collins's book *Good to Great* (New York: HarperCollins, 2001).

Not only do great organizations differentiate themselves, but they are also led and managed by individuals who had to learn to differentiate themselves personally. That's why this book begins with how individuals have used the 10 keys to leadership.

Great organizations like Abbott Laboratories have been able to change how they are differentiated when one of their three success factors is no longer at the optimum. Often, however, organizations and individuals keep doing what they are best at and passionate about despite overwhelming evidence that what they are doing is no longer driving their economic and creative engines. For an example, see the sidebar on IBM.

Three Key Questions

Some people and organizations choose where they search for opportunity by weighing available alternatives—as if they were solving problems. But the great achievers have taken a better approach, analyzing areas of opportunity and asking themselves:

- What am I most passionate about?
- What can I do far better than others?
- What can bring me the highest rewards?

Each of these questions captures one differentiating factor. Let's consider each question in the light of a modern success story.

What Am I Most Passionate About?

In 1968, two boys, Bill Gates and Paul Allen, were intrigued with a computer terminal that had been installed in their high school. They began to devote long hours learning to operate it. Within a year, the 12-year-old Gates had written a small computer program to play tic-tac-toe. Although it took longer to play than it did with pencil and paper, Gates was fascinated with the program.

Within a few years, the boys had learned enough to make money doing small programming jobs for local firms. They invested the money they made into more computer terminal time. Both of them had so much passion for computer programming that they spent all their free time doing it (figure 1-2).

> IBM went through an agonizing period in the early 1980s, when the computing power of small, low-cost computers began to rise rapidly, and other companies were providing integrated solutions to their customers. IBM's leaders had a passion for building large, mainframe computers, and they did it better than anyone else. So they continued to focus nearly all their resources on mainframes. They didn't transform IBM into an integrated-solutions provider until it suffered large financial losses.

Figure 1-2. Bill Gates and Paul Allen in 1983 just after signing a contract
to write the MS-DOS software for IBM (© Corbis)

What Can I Do Far Better Than Others?

During those early days at the high school computer terminal, Gates realized he was not only good at computer programming; he could be far better at it than anyone else. Like him, most of the great innovators and achievers have discovered from experience what they do well and what gives them uniqueness and a competitive advantage compared with others.

Recent research by Marcus Buckingham and Curt Coffman indicates that the most successful managers focus on discerning what their staff members do better than others and then placing them where they'll perform best. This research analyzed 80,000 interviews with managers, conducted as part of a Gallup Poll; it's reported in Buckingham and Coffman's book *First, Break All the Rules* (New York: Simon & Schuster, 1999).

What Will Bring Me the Highest Rewards?

In 1972, Gates and Allen bought one of the early microprocessors and tried unsuccessfully to program it to run the computer language BASIC. So they programmed the microprocessor to measure traffic data. The traffic machine worked but was not a commercial success. Through these failures, they began to believe that they could make money in the computer business if they just found the right application. Then, in January 1975, they discovered that Altair was advertising a small $400 computer. They feared that the computer revolution had started without them.

But they noticed that the advertised computer had rows of switches on its front plate that had to be programmed by hand, meaning that it didn't come with any useful programs. They immediately told Altair that they had a BASIC program that would run on its machine. Then they worked around the clock to prove they could actually do it. Gates wrote the BASIC4 program while Allen found an ingenious way to test the program on a large mainframe computer.

Then Allen flew to Altair's headquarters in Albuquerque, New Mexico. In the presence of the owner of Altair, he held his breath as he loaded the program. When the teletype printed the word "ready," he typed in "print 2 + 2." Immediately the teletype printed the answer "4."

All those watching knew that they'd just witnessed the birth of a personal computer. Altair's owner was ready to make a deal. Gates and Allen were in on the ground floor.

They chose where to search for opportunity based on what they could be rewarded for doing, what they had a passion to do, and what they could do better than anyone else. Allen quit his job at Honeywell, and Gates dropped out of Harvard. They named their new company Microsoft.

Life Purpose Is Woven Into Each Differentiating Factor

Purpose is a powerful driver of passion. People who find high purpose in their work also have high passion for the work. People who can do something far better than others often find high purpose in sharing their talents and expertise with others. When you are rewarded highly for what you do,

- you are able to support your family
- you can contribute to the lives of others
- you can use your resources to influence important community and world events.

The great scientist Marie Curie was driven early in life with the purpose of obtaining a Ph.D. at a time in Europe when no woman had ever been awarded one. Knowing what she was up against, she differentiated herself by choosing physics, a field for which she had a passion, in which she was far better than others, and in which she thought she might be able to get a PhD. Later in life, when she had been highly rewarded, she made it her purpose to cure cancer.

Collins found that corporations that had great performance over a 15-year period chose where they did business based on three factors:

- what they could be best at
- what they had a passion for
- what drove their economic engines.

These are the same success factors that great individual contributors have used to choose their fields of work.

The great achievers have focused first on doing the right things for success. Then they have focused on doing things right.

After determining where they have the best chances of finding success, the great achievers have devoted a great part of their time to learning the most valuable knowledge and skills in the fields or markets in which they chose to work. In doing that, they have discovered some very powerful learning processes. In other words, after they have decided where to search, their next key was to find what was best to learn and how to best learn it. The exemplary great achiever described in the second key was an exceptional learner. He used powerful learning processes to create the largest corporation on earth.

Self-Evaluation Exercise

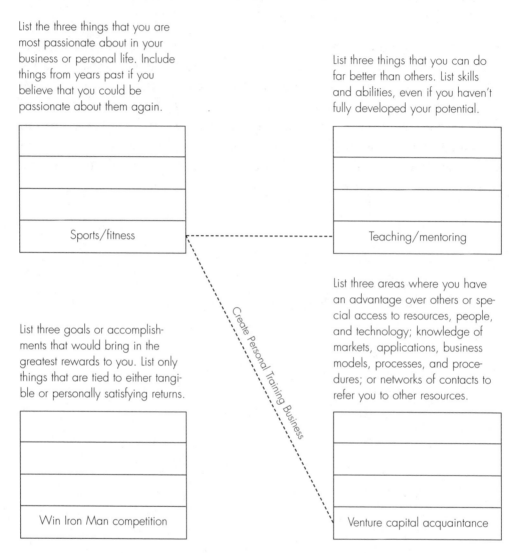

List the three things that you are most passionate about in your business or personal life. Include things from years past if you believe that you could be passionate about them again.

Sports/fitness

List three things that you can do far better than others. List skills and abilities, even if you haven't fully developed your potential.

Teaching/mentoring

List three goals or accomplishments that would bring in the greatest rewards to you. List only things that are tied to either tangible or personally satisfying returns.

Win Iron Man competition

List three areas where you have an advantage over others or special access to resources, people, and technology; knowledge of markets, applications, business models, processes, and procedures; or networks of contacts to refer you to other resources.

Venture capital acquaintance

Create Personal Training Business

Next, draw lines between all the above differentiators in each of the four categories that are related or could be combined in the pursuit of opportunity. (Note the example of personal training given here.) Then, on the lines between any two differentiators, write an opportunity that could be pursued by taking each of these distinguishing features and discovering an activity that combines both. If an opportunity can be pursued that connects three or more categories, the potential for extraordinary results is increased.

Key 2

Make the Most of Learning

*Those who want to experiment without possessing some knowledge
are like navigators who set sail without a rudder or a compass
and who are never sure where they are going.*

—Leonardo da Vinci

It was 1945, World War II was over, and the United States was adjusting to the end of rationing. Beef and butter could again be purchased in any quantities. The wartime rules allowing the manufacture of only black, white, and brown clothing were lifted, and clothes could now be purchased in many colors.

On Front Street, in the heart of the cotton town Newport, Arkansas, John Dunham owned a store with annual sales of $150,000. The Ben Franklin Store across the street was a loser, with annual sales of $70,000 and a high lease of 5 percent of sales. When he learned that a returning soldier had bought the store, he felt pity for him. So when Dunham found the young man roaming his store, checking on his prices and displays, he was glad to answer the man's seemingly endless questions.

At first, Dunham was amused by the young man's wild promotions: a popcorn machine out on the sidewalk, a Ding-Dong ice cream machine, and a sale of ladies' panties at four for a dollar. But Dunham's amusement was short-lived. In a few years, the soldier's sales exceeded his. To counter the threat, Dunham decided to lease the property next to his store and expand. But he made a mistake by discussing his plan with friends. When he drove to Hot Springs to sign the lease, he got the shock of his life. The lease had already been signed by the friendly returned soldier, Sam Walton (figure 2-1).

Figure 2-1. Sam Walton circa 1936
(Photo courtesy of Wal-Mart Corporate Communications)

Lifelong Learning

Throughout his life, Walton studied the expertise of the competition. Once, when he heard that a retail store in Minnesota had placed all its checkout registers at the front of the store instead of in each department, he traveled more than 500 miles on a bus to learn how it worked. When he introduced the practice in his stores, he found that it not only saved shopper's time; sales actually increased. His thirst for knowledge never ceased.

Years later, after Walton had already built his sprawling empire, he traveled to South Africa to learn the expertise of a small retailer who was doing exceptionally well. For 12 hours a day, as a guest of the small retailer, he visited stores, examined floor designs, checked inventories, questioned customers, and talked with vendors—taking notes all the while. He believed that anyone who was successful, even in a small way, had expertise worth learning. He also had the humility to ask others to teach him. In 2001, Wal-Mart became the largest corporation on Earth, with more than $200 billion in sales and 1 million employees.

To help you understand how the great achievers learned faster and better than others, this book often uses the word "expertise," meaning extensive knowledge and ability gained through study and experience. Walton and other great achievers found the answer to three important questions about expertise:

- Why is expertise so valuable?
- Which expertise is the most valuable?
- What are the most powerful ways to learn expertise?

Why Is Expertise So Valuable?

Popular books don't stress the importance of expertise in achieving success, but researchers agree that it's the most critical factor. Pablo Picasso referred to its value in describing an incident that took place on a sidewalk in Paris. He was sketching when a woman spotted him and asked to have her portrait done. He agreed. In minutes, she was depicted in an original Picasso. When the woman asked what she owed him, Picasso said 5,000 francs. Surprised, she protested that it had only taken three minutes. "No," Picasso told her. "It took me all my life." Picasso is quoted by Harry Beckwith, *Selling the Invisible* (New York: Warner Books, 1997).

Frederick Douglass also knew the value of expertise. In 1827, as an American slave, he was sent to live with a white plantation family. For the first time in his life, he walked on carpets instead of dirt floors and had shoes and a hat to keep him warm (figure 2-2). He no longer shared corn mush with other children from a trough on the floor. He was intrigued that the family members read books, and he begged the lady of the house to teach him how to read. One day, a few weeks into the lessons, as she was praising the boy's progress, her husband flew into a rage, telling her that she was breaking the law; if she taught the boy to read, he'd be unfit to be a slave. He said the boy should know only the will of his master.

Overhearing this, Douglass was hurt. But he also was impressed. If reading was that valuable, he wanted to read. From that day on, he hoarded scraps of printed paper as if they were gold. While he worked long hours in a factory, he studied newspapers

Figure 2-2. Portrait of Frederick Douglass, 1850 (© Corbis)

that he nailed up at reading height. At the age of 13 years, he purchased his first book, *The Columbian Orator*, with money he earned by shining shoes. He believed learning was an opportunity rather than a chore.

Douglass escaped from slavery and, at great risk, he toured the United States, speaking for emancipation. He wrote a best-selling book about life as a slave and founded the first black-owned newspaper. During the Civil War, President Abraham Lincoln sought his counsel on the Emancipation Proclamation. In 1871, he promoted the passage of constitutional amendments banning slavery, making citizens of all people born in the United States, and outlawing racial discrimination in voting.

Expertise set Douglass free, and he set others free. The sidebar highlights the opinions of some major researchers and practitioners on the importance of expertise. For more on Douglass, see Joel A. Rogers, *World's Great Men of Color* (New York: Touchstone, 1947).

The Importance of Expertise

Howard Gardner, the creativity guru from Harvard, analyzed the talents, personalities, and work habits of Albert Einstein, Sigmund Freud, Mohandas Gandhi, Martha Graham, T. S. Eliot, Igor Stravinski, and Pablo Picasso; see Howard Gardner, *Creating Minds* (New York: Basic Books, 1993). In all cases, their creative breakthroughs took place after 10 years of study and the acquiring of experience—time in which they devoted almost their whole beings to their chosen fields.

Teresa Amabile, a leading creativity researcher, says, "Being creative is like making a stew. The essential ingredient, like the vegetables and meat in the stew, is expertise in a specific area. No one is going to do anything creative in nuclear physics unless that person knows something, and probably a great deal, about nuclear physics." She is quoted in *The Creative Spirit*, by Daniel Goleman, Paul Kaufman, and Michael Ray (New York: Penguin Books, 1992).

The prolific inventor Jacob Rabinow once said, "If you're a musician, you should know a lot about music. . . . If you were born on a deserted island and never heard music, you're not likely to be a Beethoven; . . . you may imitate birds, but you're not going to write the Fifth Symphony." He is quoted in his book *Inventing for Fun and Profit* (San Francisco: San Francisco Press, 1990).

Expertise Versus Heredity and Circumstance

Some people downplay the importance of expertise. They say that leaders are born to lead or have certain personality traits that make them good leaders. Some say that leaders become great because they're in great organizations or because of the situations in which they are leading. They use Winston Churchill as an example of a leader who became great because World War II occurred during his term of leadership.

The fact is that Churchill had been an influential military and government leader for 35 years before World War II. He became a national hero in 1899 for his daring leadership and his escape from imprisonment in South Africa. He was elected to Parliament for 40 years in a row, beginning in 1924. He was an expert on history and saw the future as few have. He warned the world about Hitler many years before Hitler's evil was apparent to others. In the late 1930s, Churchill vigorously and publicly opposed those who appeased Hitler by allowing him to take portions of Poland and Czechoslovakia.

As World War II broke out in Europe, Churchill was asked to serve as leader of the British Admiralty. He devoted himself to building up the navy and developing anti-submarine warfare. When Arthur Neville Chamberlain resigned, King George asked Churchill to become prime minister and to lead the British war effort. By this time, Churchill was an expert on government, the military, and leadership. His expertise proved crucial to winning the war.

The "great achievers" whose lives are highlighted here are all giants. How do we know that the same 10 keys are important to people who aren't giants—who make smaller but still valuable contributions? Do these keys really apply to everyone?

To answer this question, we researched many lesser-known achievers. But we held to a rule. To be sure that the keys stand the test of time—that they will be valid 100 years from now—we studied only those who had sustained success for at least 10 years.

Expertise and Opportunity

Although less well known, Vito Pascucci qualifies as an achiever. In high school, he learned to repair musical instruments. When he went into the army during World War II, the great bandleader Glenn Miller heard of his repair skills and had him assigned to his band. After Paris was liberated toward the end of the war, his job was to drive a truck with all the band's instruments to Paris. Miller flew. Pascucci and Miller planned to visit musical instrument manufacturers while they were in Paris, so they could open music stores across the United States after the war. It was Pascucci's dream of a lifetime (figure 2-3).

Figure 2-3. Glenn Miller and Vito Pascucci (left to right) in England during World War II. (Photograph courtesy of Leon Pascucci.)

When Pascucci reached Paris, he was devastated by the news that Miller's plane was missing—lost at sea. The dream was over.

When the shock wore off, Pascucci visited instrument companies himself. During one visit to a factory, his life took another turn. His tour guide told him that the company wanted to sell instruments in the United States, but instruments lost their performance during sea shipment. Pascucci told the guide to give the wooden parts time to stabilize in the new atmosphere in the United States. If they were then reassembled, adjusted, and tested, he was sure they could be restored to factory specifications. Impressed, the guide invited him home for dinner. The guide turned out to be the instrument manufacturer's son, Leon Leblanc.

After the war, Pascucci set up a Leblanc branch office in the United States. By day, he restored instruments shipped from France to factory condition. By night, he wrote to retailers and distributors. Sales grew so fast that the French factory couldn't keep up. So it had Pascucci build a plant in the United States. Years later, he bought a controlling interest in the entire company. The Leblanc firm has won every award for musical instruments and today is a world symbol of performance and quality.

Pascucci's success again shows the importance of expertise in finding and seizing opportunities. He found the opportunity with Glen Miller because he was an expert in his work. Misfortune took that opportunity away. But the Leblancs offered Pascucci another great opportunity because he had the expertise. The great achievers like him have considered expertise so important that they've devoted themselves to becoming "expert insiders."

Becoming an Expert Insider

Many people say that insiders are too biased to create new ideas; that new ideas always come from outsiders. We have found that this isn't true. They called Einstein an outsider because he didn't work with any of the great physicists of his time before he developed his Special Theory of Relativity. But he graduated from the Swiss Polytechnic and was more of an expert in his field than any person alive when he made his breakthrough.

Edison was considered an outsider because he finished only the fourth grade and wasn't part of the existing lighting market. But before his team invented electric lighting, he and his team had extensively studied what other pioneers in electric lighting had done, and they knew they could invent a light that would be far superior to anything that had been invented. In other words, they knew more than anyone else.

Bill Gates was considered an outsider. But he and Paul Allen knew more about personal computer software than anyone else in the world at the time.

In other words, Einstein, Edison, and Gates were expert insiders.

Power Insiders

A second type of insider, the "power insider," has the power and control of the resources in a field but seldom comes up with the big innovations—according to the research that Burton Klein did on 20th-century innovations; see his *Dynamic Economics* (Cambridge, Mass.: Harvard University Press, 1977).

Research done by John Jewkes and his colleagues also revealed that expert insiders who were "outside" their industries came up with almost all the big innovations in the 18th and 19th centuries; see *The Sources of Invention*, by John Jewkes, David Sawers, and Richard Stillerman (London: Macmillan, 1960). In other words, while less successful people around them were waiting to win the life lottery, the great innovators knew that the chances of finding and seizing great opportunities are higher for those who have high expertise in their fields.

The Need to Spend Time Learning

In writing this book, we received much feedback about how most people don't want to hear about spending a lot of time learning. Many people are looking for drive-through success. People would rather hear that the power and creativity are within them, and they just have to find ways to release and harness them. Although it is true that power and creativity are within us, we have to develop the expertise to tap into them. If someone lacks expertise in a field, he or she has little to release to that field.

Certainly, Einstein, Gates, and Abbott Laboratories spent a great deal of time in preparation. But even small investments in preparation pay off. If Edison had spent a little time studying the market for an electric vote recorder, he wouldn't have wasted his time and other people's money on it. He learned the value of a small amount of preparation when he failed. From then on, he spent a lot of his time learning.

The great achievers spent a lot of time learning about their work and their markets. But they also knew that the amount of expertise they needed was greater than they could ever achieve with ordinary learning processes. Although it's hard to believe the great achievers thought anything was beyond them, they knew they weren't superhuman. They saw the obstacles and overcame them.

Overcoming the Obstacles to Gaining Expertise

The available expertise of any field is large and growing rapidly. Tens of thousands of books and articles are published each year. Yet people have the same 24 hours a day and no better minds than those who lived in Michelangelo's time. With ordinary approaches, no one can hope to become an expert insider.

You may argue that people live twice as long, on the average, and have information systems and communication technology that the earlier great achievers didn't have. But today's world is more complex and demanding. Examine how much time you spend expanding your expertise in your field. To repeat, the great achievers knew the importance of expertise for success and they knew that the amount of expertise in their fields was greater than they could ever learn. So they "leveraged" their time, brainpower, and resources. Figure 2-4 shows a graphical representation of the total expertise of any field versus the high-leverage expertise and ability to learn. The figure assumes that not all processed expertise will be high leverage—note the lower circle in the diagram.

High-Leverage Focus

The great achievers focused on the expertise that was most valuable in their work or their markets. In other words, they always set themselves up to get the largest rewards for the time and resources they spent. Their thinking was based on the ancient principle of mechanical leverage. The earliest humans discovered how to use mechanical leverage to go beyond their physical limitations. They found that a person easily could lift a one-ton weight with a well-designed lever. Archimedes first put the principle in writing in 200 B.C. To make his point, he said, "Give me a lever and a place to stand and I will move the earth."

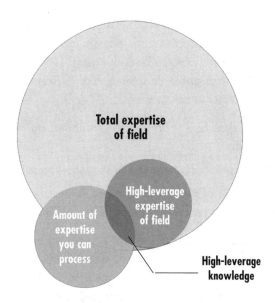

Figure 2-4. Total expertise versus high-leverage expertise.

In the same way, the great achievers discovered the mental equivalent of the mechanical lever. They looked for where they could focus the smallest amount of time and resources to produce the maximum gains toward their goals. This took them beyond the limits of the normal human mind and of their personal time and resources.

Which Expertise Is the Most Valuable?

Sam Walton had the ability to identify the expertise that gave him the best chance of success, compared with the time and effort he had to spend acquiring it. After he had multiple stores, he decided that his company needed expertise in computers and that someone else could achieve that better than he could. He attended an IBM class on information technology, with the purpose of hiring a person from the class who could lead that effort, and he did.

We define the most valuable expertise as high-leverage expertise and, fortunately, it's only a small part of all the expertise in an area of work. But how does a person identify the high-leverage expertise of a particular field? See the sidebar for the example of trout fishing.

Both Leonardo da Vinci and Thomas Jefferson used high-leverage thinking by seeking expertise from masters in their fields. In his book *Leonardo* (New York: Knickerbocker Press, 1992; from which the quotation at the start of the chapter is taken), Roger Whiting quotes memos that da Vinci wrote to himself:

- "Ask a maestro how mortars are positioned on bastions by day and by night."
- "Get the master of mathematics to show how to square a triangle."
- "Find a master of hydraulics and get him to show how to repair, and the costs of repair, of a lock, canal, and mill."

In 1769, Jefferson was elected to the Virginia Assembly. Although he was already a well-educated man, one of his first acts was to order and read 14 books, written by the giants in the field, on the theory and practice of government. For more on Jefferson, see *Thomas Jefferson* by Willard Sterne Randall (New York: HarperCollins, 1993).

When we asked masters which expertise gave the highest leverage in their fields or markets, they said it was

- the fundamental concepts and principles
- the significant patterns
- the best processes, tools, and technology.

Let's consider each type of expertise.

Fundamental Concepts and Principles

Although the tools of carpenters have changed, the fundamental concepts and principles of carpentry are the same as they were for the ancient builders of ships and buildings. Even 1,000 years ago, master carpenters knew how to design roof trusses that would support a roof for 1,000 years without sagging.

Yet the key principles of medicine have changed greatly. Doctors no longer believe that draining the blood from a patient will eliminate a disease. But 150 years ago, doctors didn't sterilize before an operation because they believed that tiny germs couldn't kill people.

Edison always identified the fundamental concepts and principles he had to learn to invent his newest product, and he either learned them himself or hired an expert

If you want to become expert in trout fishing, you might hire a trout-fishing guide. The guide may teach you to hold a tiny net at the surface of the fast-moving water to find the most frequent insect, because the trout will always bite on the one that's most plentiful. Trout are high-leverage thinkers. Then the guide will give you an artificial fly that matches the most plentiful insect and teach you to cast upstream of the fast-moving water and to let the fly drift naturally. This is high-leverage expertise that would take a long time to learn on your own. A good book written by an expert may also do the job, minus the feedback from the guide who is there to correct your technique when you snag a bush or lose a biting fish because you didn't set the hook properly.

insider. Scientists of Edison's time said that light bulbs would never be used in the home because they used too much current and there was not enough copper in the world to carry the current to millions of homes. So Edison hired Francis Upton, a Princeton physicist, who knew the design principles needed to produce a low-current filament for a light bulb. Edison and Upton came up with a design that used only 1 percent of the original current. The design concepts they developed are still used today to make incandescent light bulbs.

Significant Patterns

The architecture researcher Christopher Alexander concludes that patterns are the sources of creative power in individuals who use them; without patterns, they cannot create anything. He says that a person who has a great deal of experience building houses has a rich and complex set of patterns from which to work. If you take those patterns away, the builder can perform only simple tasks. For more on this, see Christopher Alexander, *The Timeless Way of Building* (New York: Oxford University Press, 1979).

Those who learn the patterns of stock prices or the pattern that a wide receiver runs on a football pass play see a rich world of relationships and designs that others cannot see. The Velcro fastener was inspired by the pattern that allows seed burrs to stick to trousers. The inventor of the pull-top tab for soda and beer cans was inspired by the way a banana peels.

Leonardo da Vinci advised that we take the time each day to study the world around us for its patterns.

Best Processes, Tools, and Technologies

A master carpenter also has a vast storehouse of processes for shaping wood, such as sawing, drilling, routing, and sanding. Once a carpenter visualizes what he wants to construct, he will select and use the best process he knows and the best tools he has for each step in the construction. Most modern companies do not survive unless they adopt the best lean processes, tools, and technologies in their manufacturing areas and computer-aided design technologies in their product-development areas.

Creatively Combining Expertise to Create New Products

Expertise is growing so fast that few people today can become expert insiders in more than one work area at a time. However, many major innovations are the result of creatively combining the expertise of many fields. For instance, to create a light bulb, Edison hired experts in glassblowing, vacuum technology, chemistry, physics, machining, magnetics, model making, and electricity. He managed this team of experts to creatively combine their expertise.

To create computer-animated motion pictures, such as *Toy Story*, *A Bug's Life*, and *Monsters Inc.*, Pixar's founder, Ed Catmull, brought together expert artists along with experts in computer programming and animation (as related by Gardiner Morse in "Conversation with Ed Catmull," *Harvard Business Review*, August 2002). Each person was cross-trained in the tools that Pixar uses and in filmmaking, sculpting, drawing, painting, and improvisation.

Finding the Sources of High-Leverage Expertise

The great masters sought other masters to identify which concepts, principles, patterns, processes, and tools were most valuable in their fields or markets. They read the writings of the masters, attended their lectures, and worked with them. They hired or collaborated with people who had great expertise.

Some people say it's not what you know but whom you know. Our research says the expression should read "It's not only what you know but whom you influence." Many who were in the right place at the right time didn't see an opportunity because they lacked expertise in their field. Others knew the right people but lacked expertise in influencing others. You need both expertise in your field and expertise in human behavior. Edison had expertise in electromechanical invention and in marketing his inventions through the press. Colonel Sanders had expertise in frying chicken and in influencing people to buy franchises.

We realize that some young people may be skeptical about formal education when they know that Bill Gates dropped out of Harvard to start Microsoft. But they should realize that at age 11, Gates began his preparation to become one of the most knowledgeable people on earth in personal-computing software. He invested thousands of hours in learning the expertise he would need. By the time he dropped out of Harvard, he was highly prepared. Attending universities, technical schools, and vocational schools and working with masters are still the best ways to rapidly gain high-leverage expertise. However, management is a particularly difficult field in which to discern high-leverage expertise.

The High-Leverage Expertise of Management

Management is complex work, and mastering its expertise is difficult. Peter F. Drucker defines high-leverage management expertise as the capability to do these things:

- Make people capable of joint performance.
- Make their strengths effective and their weaknesses irrelevant.
- Enable the enterprise and each of its members to grow and develop as needs and opportunities change.
- Build performance into the organization—think through, set, and exemplify objectives, values, and goals.

For more, see Drucker's *The Essential Drucker* (New York: Harper Business, 2001).

Most executive managers began as individual contributors and then learned the expertise of each of the roles they had as they rose to higher responsibilities. They practiced what they learned, and they analyzed their successes and failures.

Does Too Much Focus Limit Us?

Some people say that when we focus too much, we become narrow thinkers. They say we should be generalists. We agree that it's valuable to have knowledge of many fields and markets, but our research indicates that to find great opportunity, you should be a master of at least one or two. Edison and Walton had to learn many types of expertise to build great companies, but each of them had to achieve expertise in at least one field or market area before they broke through to greatness. With Edison, it was electromechanical invention; with Walton, it was discount retailing.

What Are the Most Powerful Ways to Learn Expertise?

Even when they focused on learning the high-leverage expertise of their fields or markets, the great achievers knew that they were still limited by time and the limits of their minds. So they found four powerful learning processes that allowed them to make the most of their limits:

- Devote quality time to learning.
- Manage the thoughts that occupy your mind.
- Use deep processing.
- Learn in the pursuit of opportunity.

These learning processes, of course, may not turn you into an Einstein. But without them, even Einstein wouldn't have turned into an Einstein. He had a fine mind, but many fine minds never find greatness. It's useful to look in detail at each of the powerful learning processes.

Devote Quality Time to Learning

The next great learner, Bruce Jenner, was a master of the process of devoting quality time to learning. In the 1972 Olympics, after placing 10th in the decathlon, he was watching a Russian receive the gold medal. Although disappointed after years of preparation, he asked himself what it would take to stand at the top of that platform.

Jenner decided to take every second of every day for the next four years and do only what would prepare him to win the Olympics. From then on, he used every spare moment to prepare—even placing a hurdle near his kitchen table so that he could rehearse jumping hurdles in his mind as he ate his meals.

At the 1976 Olympics, Jenner won the gold medal by the largest margin in history and set a new world record. This is an example of the ultimate in mind focus, and the ultimate in making the most of our limited time as humans. For more on Jenner, see his book *Finding the Champion Within* (New York: Simon & Schuster, 1996).

All the great achievers have been acutely aware of the limits of their time. When the billionaire Bill Gates was asked what he could want more of, he said, "More time." To get beyond the limits of time, we must find ways to increase the time we devote to learning and we must focus our whole beings on learning—as Jenner did.

There are major differences between the time management of the great achievers and those who accomplished less. Bill Gates also said, "My success in business has largely been the result of my ability to focus on long-term goals and ignore short-term distractions." For more on Gates, see *Bill Gates* by Jonathan Gatlin (New York: Avon Books, 1999).

> *Everything requires time. It is the only truly universal condition. All work takes place in time and uses up time. Yet most people take for granted this unique, irreplaceable, and necessary resource.*
>
> —Peter F. Drucker

Fortunately, preparing to find most opportunities won't take the devotion of a Jenner or an Einstein. However, it takes thousands of hours of study and experience to become a sought-after doctor, executive, chef, plumber, or teacher. The greater the opportunities we seek, the more time we must devote to preparation. Great opportunities seldom are found by the unprepared.

Because the great achievers realized the long-term benefits of preparation better than others, and also knew that they had little time, they devoted quality time to learning. To devote quality time to learning, you need to place learning high on your list of priorities; increase the percentage of time you devote to learning; focus completely when learning; and apply what you learn, measure the results, and relearn.

The second powerful learning process is more difficult to master.

Manage the Thoughts That Occupy Your Mind

Our brains can store unlimited knowledge and combine it in unlimited ways. They can process millions of subconscious thoughts per second. So why does it take more than 5,000 hours of study and experience to become a master plumber or machinist, 10,000 hours of education and experience to become a valuable knowledge worker, and far more than 10,000 hours of preparation for a career in law or medicine? If our brains are infinitely powerful, we need to understand why it takes so long.

It is often said that we use less than 10 percent of our brains and that if we could learn to use the rest, we would greatly increase our ability to think and create. The fact is that more than 90 percent of each brain directs billions of unconscious actions that take place in the daily routines of living. Picking up a cup of espresso, bringing it to your mouth, sipping, and returning the cup to its saucer require millions of small electrical and chemical reactions that are coordinated in the brain. Complex tasks, such as driving an automobile and hitting a golf ball, require the coordinated action of dozens of subsystems in the brain. Even the great achievers couldn't use those parts of their brains effectively for thinking and creating. But 10 percent of their brains was enough, because they knew how to use that 10 percent well. There are at least three main reasons it takes so long to learn expertise.

One thought at a time. The first reason it takes so long to become an expert is that a brain can process only one conscious thought at a time. This is apparent to us when we forget what we just read or heard because another thought has entered our consciousness. We think of multiple things by alternating attention among them. We must store each thought and return to it a short time later—as if we're pushing pause and play buttons on multiple mind recorders.

One thought per second. The second reason it takes so long to learn expertise is that a conscious mind can process only about one thought per second, while the subconscious is processing thousands of thoughts per second.

Subminds. The third reason for the long time it takes to learn is that our brains have hundreds of "subminds" operating below consciousness. When you overhear a conversation with the word "horrible" in it, see an attractive person, or think of something worrisome that your boss said, your submind goes into action. Brain researchers say that our subminds act independently, outside our conscious minds, and each wants to be the center of our conscious attention. (See the sidebar on Groucho Marx for an example of how subminds can intrude.) And for more on these topics, see *The Evolution of Consciousness* by Robert Ornstein (New York: Touchstone/Simon & Schuster, 1991) and *The Society of Mind* by Marvin Minsky (New York: Simon & Schuster, 1985).

Like the thought that entered Groucho's mind, our subminds intrude like thieves in the night. They distract us and sap our productivity. They produce chemicals that excite and depress us. When they dominate our actions, we ignore preparation and decrease our chances of finding great opportunities in the future. We are so attracted by the exciting parts of our worlds that we don't spend time creating our futures.

In a scene from a Groucho Marx movie, Groucho plays the leader of a small country that's close to war. In the scene, Groucho is about to meet the ambassador of the other country. He's confident that his peace offer will be accepted. But then Groucho begins talking to himself as he paces back and forth. "What if he snubs me by not shaking my hand? How will that look to my people? Why that cheap, no-good swine; he won't get away with it." By the time the ambassador arrives, Groucho is fuming. His first words to the ambassador are, "So, you refuse to shake hands with me!" He slaps the ambassador and starts a war.

If you want to get better control of the thoughts that enter your mind, you must learn to catch the uninvited intruders as they enter the brain. For example, any fire or crime you may hear about can grab your attention. You may want to find out if the police caught someone and, if they did,

- why he or she did it
- what kind of person he or she was
- what happened at the trial.

If you want to be in control of your time, you must track intrusions into your mind until you identify the top intrusion for a week. Then you must catch that intrusion and stop it each time it intrudes. This is difficult to do when modern media is swirling about us, competing for our attention while the expertise of any single area or field or market is increasing rapidly.

More than our grandparents, we must control what we allow into our minds, as Mihalyi Csikszentmahayli explains in *Creativity* (New York: HarperCollins, 1996). The great achievers could focus—they could choose to have only valuable thoughts in their minds.

As this book was being written, we received feedback that we made the keys seem like a big investment of time. The question was whether anyone could follow these keys if he or she is already busy with a job, a family, and other commitments.

Yet to find great opportunity, we must believe as the great achievers did that investment in learning brings large future benefits and increases opportunities. By using the preparation keys of the great achievers, whatever time the person spends on learning moves him or her rapidly on the path to opportunity. Somehow, we must carve out more time each day and devote it to learning our fields or markets. Even small amounts of time increase our chances of success.

Another question raised about the keys was where recreation fits in.

Recreation is good for the spirit. But a serious musician will spend a Sunday afternoon with a musical artist instead of attending a baseball game because he knows the value of preparation or he loves music first. To willingly devote the time to our fields or markets, we must choose work for which both learning and working are recreational. If you're in work for which you have no passion, you must either change what you do or learn to love it.

The next learning process is the most powerful one: deep processing.

Use Deep Processing

To understand deep processing, it is important to first consider the popular method of "memory recall." The brain is limited in its ability to store, combine, and recall memories. To get around these limitations, the early Greeks developed memorization techniques that are now universally taught. These techniques were made popular because of a terrible accident that took place at a banquet in 471 B.C. After reciting poetry to the assembled group, the poet Simonides was called outside to meet some men. While he was outside, the concrete roof of the banquet hall collapsed, crushing the guests within. When he was asked if he remembered any of the positions and names of the guests, Simonides reproduced the entire guest list and where each guest was seated.

When Simonides explained how he used a system of mental images based on the location of each guest around the table, his learning methods immediately became popular. Although the use of visual images for memorization is effective—to some degree—for almost everyone, some people remember better what they hear, what they touch, or what they feel emotionally. It is important to use memorization techniques that are best suited for you.

Although what Simonides did was remarkable, he was not being innovative; he was recalling images and facts. The ability to recall memories was not what enabled him to write epic poems. Rather, it was his ability to store memories so that they could be creatively retrieved later. It is important to understand the difference between recalling something and creatively retrieving it. Let's look at an example of creative retrieval.

In 1935, Edgar Kaufman asked Frank Lloyd Wright to design a small summer home for him. But after Wright visited the site and had it surveyed, he did nothing. One day, Kaufman called him and said he was 40 miles away and would like to see the design. "Come on, Edgar," Wright said. "We're ready."

Overhearing Wright's conversation, two of his primary draftsmen couldn't believe what he had promised. He had not drawn a single line. One draftsman, Edgar Tafel, detailed the scene that followed in his book *Years with Frank Lloyd Wright: Apprentice to Genius* (New York: McGraw-Hill, 1979):

> WRIGHT HUNG UP THE PHONE, WALKED TO THE DRAFTING ROOM AND STARTED TO DRAW, TALKING IN A CALM VOICE. "THEY WILL HAVE TEA ON THE BALCONY. . . . THEY'LL CROSS THE BRIDGE TO WALK INTO THE WOODS," WRIGHT SAID. PENCILS WERE USED UP AS FAST AS WE COULD SHARPEN THEM. HE ERASED, OVERDREW, MODIFIED, FLIPPING SHEETS BACK AND FORTH. THEN HE TITLED IT ACROSS THE BOTTOM: FALLINGWATER.

Two hours later, when Kaufmann arrived, Wright greeted him and showed him the front elevation. "We've been waiting for you," Wright said.

They went to lunch, and we drew up the other two elevations. When they came back, Wright showed Kaufmann the added elevations.

Wright's Fallingwater made the front cover of *Time* magazine in January 1938. The house is built on top of a waterfall that cascades through the lower level. Wright and his team were able to produce an award-winning design in a few hours because they had vast stores of expertise in their memories that had been developed over decades and which they could creatively retrieve. The key lesson here is that they didn't simply recall the memories they had stored; they retrieved new creative combinations of these memories—memories they had stored using a powerful learning tool: deep processing.

Research has shown that one's ability to creatively retrieve memories is affected primarily by how one first puts something into memory. All the great achievers used deep processing to store expertise so that they could creatively retrieve it later. They processed information deeper in their brains than less successful people did. To deep process memories the way they did, you need to:

- Relate and compare what you're learning to the expertise you already have.
- Ask yourself what is similar, what is different, what is new, what agrees with what you already know, and what does not.
- Go beyond the superficial and ask, what is the special meaning of this expertise to me, to others, and to society?
- Ask why you are better off knowing the expertise and what you can do with it.
- Question the expertise, think of its opposite, debate it with others, teach it, and review it several times in the coming days.
- Use your sight, your hearing, and your physical body to learn, but especially use the one that allows you to learn the best.
- Create images of the expertise in your mind combined with what you already know. Sketch the images or write descriptions of them.
- Learn with passion.

These findings are from *Searching for Memory: The Brain, the Mind, and the Past* by Daniel L. Schacter (New York: Basic Books, 1996). Some brain scientists, including Schacter, use the term "elaborative encoding" instead of "deep processing."

When we deep process expertise into memory, all the memories stored earlier are enriched, because the new memories interact with the old ones, and accumulated

expertise grows like ivy. So when we retrieve a deeply processed memory, we can get new, creative, valuable patterns without consciously recalling the individual memories that are combined. The subconscious mind is not bound by conscious rules, so it can make creative combinations of stored expertise that the conscious mind won't allow.

When Simonides recalled the people at the banquet, he brought individual memories to consciousness. However, when Simonides wrote great poems and when Wright designed Fallingwater, they creatively combined deeply processed memories in their subconscious minds. Then they brought the new creative combinations to the conscious level. In essence, the great achievers were innovative primarily because they had great stores of deeply processed expertise that could be creatively combined in their subconscious minds. As we will see later in the book, they also had special ways to coax their brains to combine their deeply processed expertise in new and wonderful ways.

Learn in the Pursuit of Opportunity

The fourth powerful learning process that the great achievers used was learning in the pursuit of opportunity. The researcher Edgar Dale found that, two weeks after reading, hearing, or seeing something, we remember only 10 percent of it; see "Edgar Dale's Cone of Experience," in *Education Media* by R. V. Wiman and W. C. Meierhenry (Columbus: Charles Merrill, 1969). However, if we discuss it with others, the level of retention is increased to 20 to 40 percent. Dale says that, when expertise has high meaning for us, when we have a purpose in learning it, and when we learn it directly through experience, we may remember as much as 60 percent of it two weeks later.

It has been consistently found that we learn the best and fastest when we are pursuing opportunities. Opportunity-finding and -seizing workshops are based on that principle. In these workshops, immediately after teaching the concepts and principles, it is important to help the participants find and seize the highest-leverage opportunities—whether for markets, leanness, personal development, or organizational development.

> *There are people who can recall detailed information they have only scanned and never really thought about. I'm not one of them. I have a good memory, though, for information that I've been deeply involved with or cared about.*
>
> —Bill Gates

Pursuing opportunities is the best way to learn, because a person

- learns with a purpose
- deep processes what is learned
- is directly engaged in an innovative process
- challenges his or her strengths, which increases them
- reinforces what is learned through successes and failures
- is passionate about what is being learned.

In this process, the hippocampus in the midbrain will decide to store information long term if we repeat it, if we dwell on it, or if it arouses emotion. If all three are strong, the memory may last a lifetime. This process of opportunity-driven learning is another reason that the great achievers, like Einstein and Wright, learned faster and better than others. They were always preparing for, finding, and seizing opportunities. They were in constant pursuit of opportunity.

In summary, deep processing and learning in the pursuit of opportunity are the two most effective power learning processes of the great innovators and achievers.

Secret Strategies?

Twenty years ago, when our research team was investigating what made people great, we suspected that the great achievers had secret strategies. The 10 keys could be considered secrets, not because the great achievers kept them secret but because only a few recognized their importance. Even when we began to teach adults how to apply these keys in their lives and organizations, many were skeptical. Since then, we have followed their careers and the success of their organizations. We have found that those who followed the path of these keys were more successful than those who didn't.

Once you master these powerful learning processes, you can rapidly learn the expertise of the fields of work or markets that you have chosen. Or you can use them to change jobs or start new businesses. Either way, you would identify which knowledge and skills are the most important, and then you would devote quality time to learning and practicing them. You would deep process what you learn, relating and creatively combining it with the knowledge and skills you already have. Then you would be ready to search for opportunity.

Summary of Keys 1 and 2

To summarize so far:

- First, the great achievers chose to search for opportunity where they had the best chance of finding great opportunity.
- Second, they became expert insiders by using powerful learning processes to learn the high-leverage expertise of their work.

Key 3 of the great achievers is that they learned to envision opportunity. At the beginning of the 20th century, the next master we examine envisioned a great opportunity. After her discoveries, scientists had a new view of the atom. Her story begins on the most disappointing day of her life, at the end of four years of intensive research and backbreaking labor.

Self-Evaluation Exercise

List your most valuable areas of expertise that pertain to opportunities listed in the exercises at end of the key 1 chapter and/or areas of interest to you. Write these in the left-hand column below. Expertise can be in the areas of emerging technologies, established technology, nontechnical, social, political, medical, industry specific, arts, education, and the like.

Expertise	Books	Periodicals	Courses/seminars	Experts	Internet	Other
Example Marketing a business startup	✓				✓	

For each type of expertise, list one or more ways to pursue learning it by checking the corresponding boxes to its right.

Eliminate the pursuit of low-leverage expertise: Eliminate each category above if it is an area of interest only and is not tied to substantial rewards; eliminate it if only broad knowledge is required and you have access to other experts in that category; eliminate it if there is no tangible return on effort or market need for the result of gaining expertise in this category.

Within the remaining types of expertise listed above, list one area of this field of expertise that would be most effective to learn if you could only dedicate one hour a week to learning it; these are your high-leverage areas of expertise.

Key 3

Envision Great Opportunities

"No use trying," Alice said. "One can't believe impossible things."
"I daresay you haven't had much practice," said the Queen.
"When I was your age, I always did it for half-an-hour a day.
Why, sometimes I've believed as many as six impossible things
before breakfast."

—Lewis Carroll, *Through the Looking Glass*

In 1895, Marie Curie obtained her undergraduate degree in physics from the University of Paris. As a woman at that time, she would not be considered for a doctoral degree, even though she was at the top of her class. However, she knew that if she made a breakthrough scientific discovery, she might have a chance (figure 3-1).

X-rays, a form of invisible light, had just been discovered by Wilhelm Röntgen. Using her scientific expertise, Curie predicted that the element thorium might emit invisible light. She bought large quantities of pitchblende, a naturally occurring ore that contained small amounts of thorium. She chemically separated thorium from the ore and found that it did emit an invisible light.

Then Curie made a crucial observation. After the thorium was removed, the remaining ore emitted more invisible rays per pound. Further separating the ore, she discovered a new element that she named polonium. Then there was a further surprise: The ore remaining after the extraction of polonium was thousands of times more radioactive than anything she had seen. She named it radium. To prove that it was a new element, she had to separate it from the ore.

Figure 3-1. Marie Curie, 1910 (© ImageState)

For four years, Curie crushed and chemically separated two tons of ore. As each compound was removed, the remaining material increased in radioactivity. Her husband Pierre became so excited by her findings that he abandoned the work he was pursuing and joined in her research. Then, one fateful day, after hundreds of separations, only a few ounces remained. She finished her last separation and waited anxiously as the chemicals worked.

When the reaction finished, as Curie looked for the remains in the bottom of the reactor, she found nothing. The final separation apparently had eliminated the entire compound. She was devastated. At home that night, she wrestled with thoughts of what could have gone wrong. Maybe her detractors were right. They said she was looking for something that didn't exist. She couldn't sleep. If her theory that radiation came from the center of the atom was correct, it couldn't have been destroyed chemically. In the night, she returned to the laboratory.

When Curie opened the laboratory door, it appeared as if a light had been left on. She walked quickly toward the glow. It was coming from the glass dish that held the remains of her last separation. The residue, invisible in the daylight, glowed intensely. She weighed it. It had no detectable weight, but it was highly radioactive. She was jubilant. She had extracted enough pure radium to prove that it was a new element.

In 1902, a doctoral examining board said that Curie's findings were the most significant ever presented in a doctoral thesis and awarded her the first doctoral degree ever presented to a woman in Europe. Later that year, she became the first woman to win the Nobel Prize in physics, for her discovery of radium. A few years later, she was awarded a Nobel Prize in chemistry—becoming the first person to win a Nobel Prize in two different categories. The invisible rays from radium were later used for X-ray imaging and for treating cancer.

To understand why people like Marie Curie see opportunities that others don't see, we have to answer three questions:

- What are the most creative behaviors?
- How can we see into the future?
- How can we visualize great opportunities?

Our research discovered answers to each question.

What Are the Most Creative Behaviors?

In *Creating Minds* (New York: Basic Books, 1993), Howard Gardner defines a creative person as one who regularly solves problems, develops products, or defines new questions in a way that is initially considered novel but ultimately becomes accepted. Curie had all the valuable creative attitudes and behaviors of the great opportunity finders:

- Put a high priority on creating and a low priority on consuming.
- Search for original opportunities to create.
- Learn expertise with healthy skepticism.
- Challenge assumptions and rules.
- Create a life that is a creative journey to the very end.
- Create like a child, persevere like a soldier.
- Leverage risk with expertise.

Let's discuss each of these. The most common behavior of a person with a creative mind is based on his or her priorities.

Put a High Priority on Creating and a Low Priority on Consuming

Curie was not only focused and hard working, she prioritized her use of time so that she spent most of it creating. An activity is creative if its end goal is a seized opportunity—such as creating or improving a product, service, system, or organization. For example, those who watch a football game are consumers rather than creators. The creators are the coaches, owners, players, halftime producers, television producers, directors, cameramen, ad agency staffers, and the architects and contractors who built the stadium. Creative people have more passion for creating than for consuming.

Search for Original Opportunities to Create

Early in his career, before he sculpted *David*, Michelangelo applied for work at a commercial studio. In the book *The Agony and the Ecstasy* (New York: Signet, 1961), Irving

Stone dramatizes the differences between Michelangelo's creative attitude and the attitude of the owner of the commercial studio. The owner tells Michelangelo that his deliveries are never late because he knows "within a matter of minutes how long each panel of fruit or spray of leaves will take to carve."

Michelangelo asks what happens if a sculptor thinks of "something new, . . . an idea not carved before?" The owner replies, "Sculpture is not an inventing art, it is reproductive. If I tried to make up designs, this studio would be in chaos. We carve here what others have carved before us." Michelangelo again asks him what would happen if a sculptor wanted to "achieve something fresh and different." The owner says, "That is your youth speaking, my boy. A few months under my tutelage and you would lose such foolish notions."

Of course, Michelangelo didn't take the job. He was searching for an opportunity to do original, creative work.

Learn Expertise with Healthy Skepticism

Each year, before 1952, 50,000 people were paralyzed for life with polio—the same number as were killed in automobile accidents. It was believed at the time that a person had to experience a live virus to be immune. But Jonas Salk was skeptical of that theory. So he deactivated a live virus with ultraviolet light and injected it into humans. It worked, and a vaccine was developed that decreased the cases of paralytic polio to less than 10 a year. Salk received the Presidential Medal of Freedom for his achievement.

According to studies, there's a difference in the way creative people like Salk learn. Those without a creative attitude absorb knowledge without question, but those like Salk digest knowledge with a questioning attitude. One of Salk's mentors used to ask him, "Damn it, Salk, why do you always do things differently?"

Salk saw incongruities where others saw order. He learned expertise and questioned it at the same time—questioning not so strongly as to prevent learning but strongly enough to see opportunities to create new knowledge.

Leonardo da Vinci also was a healthy skeptic. The most frequent words in his journals are "I question." He learned from the giants of the past, but he questioned them and himself as well. He accepted nothing blindly. Likewise, Galileo never took anything for granted. He once said, "In questions of science, the authority of a thousand is not worth the humble reasoning of a single individual."

Challenge Assumptions and Rules

Many automobile-racing rules were rewritten over the years because the Penske Race Team challenged them. For example, because many auto races are won by differences of seconds, shaving time from pit stops is a valuable endeavor. On one occasion, the Penske team members were trying to shave time from the 13 seconds it took to refuel during a pit stop. They knew they could increase the flow rate by increasing the fueling pressure, but pumps were illegal under the rules of the racing association (figure 3-2).

So, with the help of Sun Oil engineers, the Penske team members constructed a 20-foot tower with a large gas tank on top and a large fuel hose hanging from it. When a car drove in for refueling, they put the fuel hose in the tank, opened a valve on the fuel line, and filled the car's tank in 3.5 seconds. It was so dramatic that the driver, Mark Donohue, said he felt the back of the car suddenly sink as the fuel poured in.

But within two races, the powers that be had rewritten the rules to outlaw the Penske invention. To Penske's opponents, the rules were the rules; the Penske team saw them as boundaries to be pushed. They asked, "What don't the rules say?" The Penske team followed the first rule of innovation: There are no absolute rules. They won the Indianapolis 500 a total of 12 times—a record.

Create a Life That Is a Creative Journey to the Very End

The researcher Mihalyi Csikszentmahalyi says that creative people create their own lives; see his book *Creativity* (New York: HarperCollins, 1996). Their opportunity

Figure 3-2. Penske Race Team (© Corbis)

finding and seizing usually is rewarded, and their services are increasingly in demand. Their influence expands and leads to a wider set of opportunities. Csikszentmahalyi says they often create other sides of their personalities if that is needed to accomplish their goals. He says they learn to be objective, passionate, or both. They can be imaginative but rooted in reality as well. When they don't have the expertise needed, they collaborate with others who have it.

Creative people often create to the very end. Eight days before he died at the age of 88, Michelangelo was working on the Rondanini Pietà, a radical new work based on an entirely new concept. Pablo Casals, the great Spanish cellist, was developing and practicing a new piece of music on the day he died at the age of 97. Years after Marie Curie won the Nobel Prize, she was still creating.

Create Like a Child, Persevere Like a Soldier

Creativity is a tightrope. You must be as free as a child to create and, at the same time, you must discipline your mind. Beethoven expressed it well when he said, "To make music, one must have the spirit of a gypsy and the discipline of a soldier." The same is true for corporations; a Stanford University research team concluded from its study of public corporations of the 1980s and 1990s that corporations with the largest performance improvements developed the cultures of entrepreneurs and the discipline of soldiers; see *Good to Great* by Jim Collins (New York: HarperCollins, 2001).

If you watch small children at play, you will observe that they mostly do what's fun. When it becomes difficult, they get frustrated and begin something else. Most children are playful, curious, and full of energy—but easily distracted. They do what gives them pleasure or satisfies their curiosity. The great innovators had fun and satisfied their curiosity while focusing energetically where their efforts would produce high returns. Unlike children—who quit when the activity becomes difficult or unpleasant—the great innovators persevered.

Leverage Risk with Expertise

Each time Curie discovered new knowledge, she saw more clearly the potential of her opportunity and she increased the amount of time and energy she applied. This is not risk taking; it is expert risk taking. What Curie did would be a waste of time for anyone without her expertise.

When the great achievers didn't have the expertise they needed in their work and when they knew they would dilute their efforts by taking the time to learn it, they leveraged their risk by teaming with others who had the expertise. Steve Jobs had marketing expertise, and Steve Wosniak had expertise in using microprocessors and in creating small computer hardware. They teamed up to create Apple Computer Corporation. Gates and Allen, Hewlett and Packard—these were great pairings because they took advantage of complementary expertise.

The Creative Paradox

Throughout life, you have experiences that shape your attitudes, opinions, beliefs, and standards. You learn architectures, patterns, processes, and representations and store them in your brain. On the plus side, these help you to automatically drive to work, organize plans, and disassemble engines. They allow you to make many simple decisions and judgments without lengthy study. These patterns and principles are the sources of your creativity.

On the negative side, these fixed ways of thinking can imprison your creativity and close your windows to opportunity. You may limit the options you see, filtering anything that doesn't "fit." Even the great achievers sometimes closed their minds to opportunity. Thomas Edison and Bill Gates provide examples of this. While the rest of the world converted to alternating current, because it could be generated at low cost in large power stations and transmitted long distances efficiently, Edison opposed it. Later, after the world had passed him by, he admitted that he was wrong.

Initially, Gates wouldn't invest in Internet software because he couldn't see how he'd ever get the money back from a free network. However, when he saw that the Internet was bearing down on Microsoft like a freight train, he admitted that he was wrong and began a major effort to build Internet support into the company's software and to establish Microsoft on the Internet.

When the world changes and you continue to use models that are slow, error prone, costly, and inflexible, you become a victim of your own expertise.

Great innovators refuse to be stopped by fixed ideas. When Fred Smith started FedEx, federal law prohibited his company from carrying loads on his planes that were large enough to make money. He persuaded the government that allowing him to carry larger loads would increase competition, thus benefiting the consumer. The government changed the law, despite protests from the major airlines.

So there is a creative paradox: No significant new achievement is possible without stored expertise, nor is it possible without going beyond existing expertise.

You also must get beyond any limiting thoughts.

Finding and Changing Limiting Thoughts

Have you ever had what you thought was a great idea but then immediately put it aside, thinking "Somebody has probably already thought of that" or "It's too big for me to pull off" or "Nobody will listen to such a crazy idea"?

About 20 years ago, Judy Anderson had a great idea for starting her own business. She believed that name badges could be powerful marketing tools if they projected the right images in people's minds. She decided to quit her job and focus on her goal. She identified retail businesses for which she thought creative name badges would have a large impact. Then she designed and sent samples of name badges that would enhance their images with customers to these businesses.

Months went by with no responses. Finally, when Anderson was out of money and her credit cards were at their limits, she received a call. "How are you?" a deep voice asked. "This is Sam Walton. I have your samples on my desk, and I like your work. But it's not what I'm looking for." Anderson swallowed and said, "Mr. Walton, what do you want to say to your customers when they walk through the door?" Walton replied, "I want our customers to know that our people make the difference and that you can trust us on a handshake, and I want to have Wal-Mart on the badge."

"I'll make some new samples and send them to you in a few days," she said.

Anderson spent the rest of the day producing a variety of drawings with "Our people make the difference" and the Wal-Mart logo. She shipped the samples overnight to Walton. He loved the samples and ordered 280,000 badges. From that beginning, Anderson's company, Identification Systems, has grown into the largest custom-badge manufacturer in the world.

What if Anderson had allowed limiting thoughts, such as "Wal-Mart is too big; it won't even look at an idea from someone who isn't in the name badge business" or "If I quit my job and I fail, I won't be able to get another job as good as the one I have"?

How do we know when we have thoughts that limit us? The answer is "not easily." Most of the time, we're not aware of our limiting thoughts and beliefs. An expert in behavioral change, who helps a person or an organization find and change limiting beliefs, will begin with an analysis of recent unsatisfactory performance, lack of success, and/or unhappiness. The expert will try to determine if a limiting belief was the cause. When a limiting belief is identified, the expert helps the client to recognize situations in which that belief comes into play. Then the client is asked to rethink the reactions that led to failure and to create new positive responses.

Sometimes our beliefs limit our ability to see future threats as well as opportunities. Unless we can identify and change our reactions, we'll be limited.

Creative Organizations

Creative organizations usually are founded and led by creative individuals who have all the attitudes and behaviors discussed above and a few more. They are disciplined yet entrepreneurial, as Collins notes in *Good to Great*. The leaders of these organizations encourage open exchanges of ideas, yet they ask everyone to rally behind the opportunities that are selected for action. They set expectations of high creativity.

Creating Responsibly

Theodore Levitt, a professor emeritus at Harvard Business School, says in his article "The Innovative Enterprise" that ideas are useless unless implemented (*Harvard Business Review*, August 2002). So it's not enough just to come up with novel ideas. A person who comes up with a new idea needs to do two things:

- First, the person should understand that the leaders of organizations continually are bombarded with problems and may not welcome new ideas.
- Second, in presenting the idea, the person should include at least a minimal indication of what it involves in terms of costs, risks, labor power, time, and perhaps even specific people to carry it through.

Levitt says that this is responsible behavior, because it is easier for the executive to evaluate the idea, which increases the chances that the idea will be used.

Along with developing their creative behaviors, the masters developed their visioning abilities, which enabled them to see and create the future. Our next master anticipated what large numbers of people would want in the future and led his company to create a whole new business.

How Can We See Into the Future?

In February 1979, the aging honorary chairman of Sony Corporation, Masaru Ibuka, asked the product development department to build a small tape player so that he could listen to stereo recordings on long plane flights. The engineers modified a small tape recorder, adding stereo circuitry. When they connected it to earphones, they were surprised. Instead of a small, narrow-band sound, the sound was full and wrapped itself around the listener.

Two weeks later, Ibuka carried it on a flight and was delighted with the sound. When he returned, he gave it to the acting Sony chairman, Akio Morita, who took it home for the weekend. That Saturday evening, as Morita entertained guests for dinner, he passed the player around and invited everyone to try it. Morita laughed as each guest showed amazement.

Morita presented the player at the next executive meeting. The executives considered it a toy, so it shocked them when Morita proposed that they have it ready for sale in four months, at a time when students went on vacation. He set the price at $125. Morita was so enthusiastic and certain about it that the other executives reluctantly went along with his "crazy idea."

Sony's engineers said that they would have to manufacture 30,000 units a month to make a profit at a price of $125. The salespeople argued that they sold only 15,000 units per month of Sony's most popular tape recorder and that they could never sell a tape player that didn't record. Morita persisted and said that he would resign as chairman if the 30,000 units didn't sell. He believed that many people would buy something they could listen to privately and while running or exercising.

Sony named the new tape player the Walkman. For a month after it hit the market, there were no sales, which confirmed the predictions of the sales department. Then the sales began; there were 30,000 in the next 30 days. The Walkman made Sony a world leader. For more on Sony, see the book *Sony, the Private Life* by John Nathan (Boston: Houghton-Mifflin, 1995).

People who see into the future

- base their thinking outside the box on expertise inside the box
- analyze trends, create future needs, and set high goals
- never say it can't be done.

Base Your Thinking Outside the Box on Expertise Inside the Box

We have to go back 25 years to understand why the Walkman breakthrough was based on expertise inside the box. In 1953, when Ibuka heard that Bell Labs had invented the transistor, he realized that transistors would revolutionize electronics. So he sent Morita to America to purchase a license from AT&T to manufacture them.

With the transistor, Sony produced the first hand-held radio and led the world in miniaturization of radio products. By the time Morita had his vision for the Walkman, Sony had hired people who had expertise in miniature circuitry and had the capacity to build thousands of miniature tape recorders and radios. Sony was able to move quickly to dominate the portable tape player market because it had the engineering, manufacturing, marketing, and distribution expertise. Morita didn't create the Walkman; his organization did.

Thinking outside the box begins with concepts, patterns, principles, and processes inside the box. Out-of-the-box ideas like electric lamps, relativity, and the Walkman don't come from nothing. All the mind-freeing, brainstorming, and radical thinking won't get you out of the box with a great opportunity if you don't have expertise inside the box to bring ideas to fruition.

Analyze Trends, Create Future Needs, and Set High Goals

In *Managing for Results*, Peter F. Drucker wrote that "the best way to predict the future is to create it" (New York: Harper, 1964). Predicting opportunities is a key to creating the future, for both individuals and organizations. Organizations can analyze where their competitors are making large profits, and they can search for markets their competitors are not serving or that they are serving but would not likely defend. They can study changes in customer behavior that could be opportunities. They can then create visions to take advantage of the identified opportunities.

There was no explicit customer need for the Walkman until Morita introduced it. People thought they needed it only after they saw it. Morita created a need. Many needs that we take for granted today were not obvious in their time—see the sidebar.

Never Say It Can't Be Done

In 1714, after a fleet of British ships was sunk as a result of a navigational error, the British Board of Longitude offered a reward of £20,000 (over $1 million in today's money) to anyone who could invent a method to measure longitude while on a ship at sea. The greatest scientist of all time, Isaac Newton, emphatically stated that no clock could be invented that could keep time precisely enough to do the job and that the only way to do it was with an astronomical instrument. Forty-five years

When presented with Alexander Graham Bell's telephone, U.S. president Rutherford B. Hayes said, "It's a great invention, but who would want to use it anyway?" In 1936, *Radio Times* editor Rex Lambert said, "Television won't matter in your lifetime or mine." Sixteen years later, television was a major media player.

later, John Harrison invented a type of clock called a chronometer. It measured time so accurately that it became the standard for longitudinal measurement for two centuries until satellite global positioning systems were invented.

How Can We Visualize Great Opportunities?

The great innovators visualize opportunities that others don't see because they

- focus on opportunities first, then creatively solve problems
- sometimes set obviously unattainable goals
- find new opportunities through creative synergies
- prepare well for a breakthrough
- incubate ideas.

Focus on Opportunities First, Then Creatively Solve Problems

It's important, before going further, to explain the difference between opportunities and problems. Jonas Salk creatively solved the problem of polio, a disease that crippled and killed people. But Sam Walton, Thomas Edison, Bill Gates, Akio Morita, Marie Curie, and Harland Sanders weren't solving problems—they were finding opportunities:

- Walton recognized that many consumers were attracted to lower-priced merchandise.
- Edison knew that offices and homes would want safe, practical lighting.
- Gates saw a computer on every desktop, running his software.
- Morita envisioned students carrying their own music and privately listening to it.
- Curie knew that science would advance if the source of the mysterious rays were discovered.
- Sanders knew he had a great fried chicken recipe.

Each of these innovators first found an opportunity and then solved the problems that stood in the way of seizing it.

When Curie found the opportunity to discover a new element, she was faced with many problems. Great quantities of radioactive ore had to be acquired. Chemical processes to separate the compounds and a device to measure low-level radioactivity had to be invented. After Gates and Allen found the opportunity to create software for a personal computer, they had to solve hundreds of problems before they could seize it. After Morita found the opportunity to provide mobile entertainment for people, his company had to solve many problems to seize the opportunity.

These innovators first searched for and found opportunities. Then they identified the problems—the barriers or obstacles—that needed to be surmounted to seize the opportunities. Then they focused their time, brainpower, and resources on solving the problems that stood in the way of seizing the opportunities. When you find an opportunity and compare it with the way things currently are, you discover problems that must be solved creatively to seize the opportunity.

Many people believe that necessity is the mother of invention. They say that you should look for the greatest pain or need that people have. Necessity is *a* mother of invention, but not the only mother. True, Salk solved the problem of pain and death from polio. But was it necessary for Walton to offer discounts, for Morita to produce a Walkman, or for Curie to find radium? You could argue that Gates filled a need for a few eager computer enthusiasts, but most people didn't have the need until they saw what the software could do for them. If you simply solve the problems presented to you or try to find problems to solve, you will miss many great opportunities.

Breakthrough Opportunities

Searching for and finding breakthrough opportunities is the highest form of visioning. Breakthrough visions—like the printing press, the steam engine, wireless communication, penicillin, the transistor, the computer, and the Internet—changed the world. It's important to know how to find breakthrough opportunities so that you can make jumps in progress that leave others behind. More than any other great achiever, Michelangelo embodies the nature of breakthrough visioning.

To see Michelangelo's genius, let's visit the Galleria dell'Accademia in Florence. As you enter, you smell the odor of aged wood and tapestries. You walk through an antechamber into a long, wide hall. The sight that awaits you as you enter the hall will be permanently etched in your mind. On each side, white marble bodies of half-carved men appear to struggle to get out of the stone that holds them. At the end of the hallway, standing majestically in a stream of light from a skylight, is the sculpture of *David*.

The half-carved men on each side of the long hallway are called *The Slaves*. They show Michelangelo's remarkable expertise. Before he began to carve, he was able to see the finished form inside the stone.

Master sculptors say that Michelangelo intended to finely finish some parts and leave other parts with a rough finish. Maybe he wanted to show us in our personal prisons. As you walk down the hall, you can hear the hushed voices of the people gathered around the great statue.

The Florence Board of Works gave Michelangelo a 17-foot-high block of white marble that was so thin and so badly gouged by a previous artist that no one wanted it. All earlier masters had sculpted David "after the battle," with one foot placed triumphantly on Goliath's severed head. Michelangelo didn't believe that standing triumphant over a dead enemy was the essence of a great man. Instead, he portrayed David moments before the battle, as he studied the enemy, dealt with his fears, and focused his mind and body.

When you look up at the towering giant, you will see that his brow is furrowed with resolution and his eyes are shooting like daggers. If your reaction is like ours, you will hear yourself breathe (figure 3-3).

Michelangelo had an exceptional visioning ability:

- He was able to see in his mind a David capable of slaying Goliath.
- He was able to see clearly the completed sculpture David in the damaged stone before he began to carve.
- He saw how to remove the excess stone to free David.

Figure 3-3. Michelangelo's *David* at the Galleria dell'Accademia in Florence (© Corbis)

For more on Michelangelo, see *The Agony and the Ecstasy* by Irving Stone (New York: Signet, 1961).

Although there are many ways to set the stage for exceptional visioning, here are a few to consider:

Set Obviously Unattainable Goals

Les Wexner, a retail pioneer and founder of The Limited clothing stores, uses visioning techniques and obviously unattainable goals to push others outside normal ways of thinking. Once, while discussing the marketing of a Shetland sweater that was projected to sell 250,000 units, Wexner said to his staff of retailing experts, "Humor me for just a minute. How would we sell a million sweaters?" Everyone in the room insisted that there was "no way." The Limited had 80 stores and would have to sell an average of 12,500 sweaters per store. Wexner listened to the objections and then said, "Just pretend. What would it take?"

Then the team members formed mental images of selling a million sweaters, which would require a bigger resource base, more manufacturing plants, more colors in the assortment, a buy-one-get-one-free offer, incentives for stores, and so on. By implementing many of these ideas, they sold 750,000 Shetland sweaters—three times the original projection.

Wexner knew that you can stimulate people's ability to create visions with questions such as:

- "What would you do if you had the power to make anything happen that you wanted to happen?"
- "What would magic look like?"
- "What would the ideal solution be?"
- "What if?"
- "Why?"
- "Why not?"
- "If you had a wish . . . ?"
- "What will it take to make us great?"

Our imaginations are stretched by setting obviously unattainable goals, like Wexner's goal to sell sweaters. If goals are set so high that normal means can't achieve them, and if they're taken seriously by organizations that have the expertise, a breakthrough vision often appears.

Find New Opportunities Through Creative Synergies

The story of Wexner's team also demonstrates the value of synergy in the creative process. The team had a great deal of expertise inside each member's head. During the brainstorming and imaging sessions, each person's ideas stimulated ideas from others, and new combinations of ideas were formed.

Wexner led the team members to create big mental images that were greater than the sum of the expertise stored in their individual minds. In other words, he led them to find new opportunity through creative synergy. Brainstorming is most effective when it is done in the pursuit of an opportunity, like "selling a million sweaters."

Prepare Well for a Breakthrough

On a chilly evening in 1865, a Flemish chemist, Fredrich Kekulé, watched the patterns of flying sparks in his fireplace. As he slipped into half-sleep, he imagined that the sparks were linked in a circle, like snakes biting their own tails. He woke with a picture of hydrogen and carbon atoms in a ring and realized that this was a likely molecular structure for benzene.

Many decades after Kekulé's death, other scientists finally accepted his description of the benzene structure. People who write about creativity often use Kekulé's vision to show that visions happen like a magician's "poof." Actually, however, the moment of illumination comes only after long-term preparation and incubation. Before Kekule saw the benzene ring in the fire, he was a professor of chemistry for nine years. He had extensive expertise in atomic-bonding principles and the patterns of chemical compounds. This story is related by Graham Wallas in *The Art of Thought* (New York: Harcourt Brace, 1926).

There also is a period of intense, short-term preparation in the days, weeks, and months preceding the breakthrough. During this period, the focus is usually narrowed to a specific area of opportunity, such as Curie's focus on finding radium and Edison's focus on a practical filament. So the lesson is: Prepare well if you want a "poof."

In summary, during long-term preparation, the mind is stocked with work expertise and opportunity-finding expertise. During short-term preparation, the specific area of opportunity is deeply studied and analyzed.

Incubate Ideas

Incubation is a period of time in which an intent or a goal in an area of opportunity percolates with all the long-term and short-term expertise stored in the subconscious.

Breakthroughs often are described by their creators as mental images that occur after periods of incubation. Einstein imagined that he was riding on a beam of light and asked: If I were going at the speed of light, would the light reflected from my face be able to get back to me so that I could see myself in a mirror? His answer led to his theory of relativity. Beethoven once said, "I always have a picture in mind when I'm composing."

Scientists say that we don't see the world around us as it is. Instead, we take the pieces that our optical systems collect and create images with them. We all have the mystical ability to create images. The *American Heritage Dictionary* defines "vision" as "a mental image produced by the imagination"; it defines "imagine" as "to form a mental picture or image"; and it defines "see" as "to have a mental image of, to visualize, to understand." All these definitions are related to your ability to create mental images. So if you want to improve your chances of creating breakthroughs, you should improve your ability to create mental images.

Once you allow potential opportunities to creatively percolate in your mind, illumination often occurs when you're not directly trying to see. It usually happens when you're at the edge of consciousness, in a near-dream state. It's as if the goal becomes a spotlight, sweeping through the caves of your unconscious mind, locating and combining bits and scraps until it finds answers.

Often, after long deliberation, an insight comes suddenly when you're not consciously searching. It may come in the midst of a long drive or walk, in the shower or bath, or on a vacation. It comes to the surface because reducing signal levels to your brain through relaxation increases your access to your subconscious mind. That's why creative people get away from the quest and do something relaxing or diversionary.

Einstein's sister said that, when he had a deep physics problem on his mind, he'd play the violin. Often, while playing his violin, he'd suddenly come to a stop and declare, "Now I've got it." Edison as well as Einstein used the same trick to access the subconscious: After allowing a problem to percolate in his mind for a while, each would sit in a chair with his hands hanging down, holding balls or rocks. When he dozed and dropped a ball or a rock, he'd jot down the first ideas that came to him.

Of course, each person must search for his or her own incubation techniques. Keep in mind that the incubation phase will not produce a vision without the expertise that comes from good preparation and good goal focus.

Once you have honed your knowledge and skills through experience and have developed your visioning techniques, you and your organization will find many opportunities. To maximize your chances of success, you will need ways to sort out and choose only the opportunities that will produce the highest level of success for the time, effort, and resources you must spend to seize them. The next master is the role model for key 4, high leverage.

 Self-Evaluation Visioning Exercise

A. If there were two things that you could wish for in your business and know that they would be granted by the following Monday, what would they be?

B. If there were two things that you could wish for in your career and know that they would be granted by the following Monday, what would they be?

C. Can you envision what it would take in the real world to make your A and B wishes come true? If you can envision what it will take, what is the first step?

Key 4

Choose High-Leverage Opportunities

*My job is to put the best people on the biggest opportunities
and the best allocation of dollars in the right places.*

—Jack Welch, quoted in *Jack Welch and the GE Way* by Robert Slater

One day on her lunch hour, Cheryl Krueger was walking in Manhattan when she saw a line of people wrapped around a street corner. The line ended at David's Cookies, which was selling lumpy, moist, delicious cookies reminiscent of her grandmother's.

Krueger had learned from her grandma how to make such cookies, so when she discovered that David's Cookies was selling franchises, she arranged to meet the owner. In a 20-minute meeting, she discovered that he wanted a franchise fee of $250,000 as well as 10 percent of the gross and that Krueger would have to buy all her cookie dough from him and pay for the shipping.

On the plane back to Columbus, Ohio, her home town, Krueger pictured the people standing in line. The cookie business would give her control of her life. But, after a hard analysis of the numbers, she calculated that she would have to sell a million dollars worth of cookies a year to make a profit. She began to wonder what she would be getting for the franchise costs. From her creative marketing expertise came the question: Did the name David's Cookies mean anything in Columbus? She spent the weekend asking people if David's Cookies meant anything to them. None of them knew the name.

A Business Idea Is Born

So Krueger created a business plan for her own company, Cheryl&Co, and approached the banks. The banks asked why people would buy cookies when they could bake them. She told them that many women were busy with careers and weren't baking much anymore. When the banks turned her down, she decided to finance the business herself.

For three years after she opened her first Cheryl&Co store, Krueger continued working in New York as a clothing company executive. Each Friday, she flew to Columbus, worked in her store over the weekend, and returned to New York on a flight early Monday morning. When the first store could support her, she quit her executive job and opened a second store.

As the number of stores increased, Krueger found a valuable opportunity to create a central baking operation to supply all the Cheryl&Co stores. That led to another opportunity. The retail dessert business was highly seasonal, and she did not like to lay off employees during the off-peak periods in her bakery. So, to level out her bakery orders, she sold private-label desserts to restaurants that served desserts all year long, such as Bob Evans, Ruby Tuesday's, and Max & Erma's. Then a few travel agencies began giving her cookies to airline representatives. The airlines liked the cookies and asked her to wrap them individually for their passengers.

Today, Cheryl&Co supplies cookies to many companies, such as Delta Airlines, US Airways, The Limited, and the Walt Disney Company. When Hallmark decided to become the premier gift company, it not only chose Cheryl&Co as its dessert supplier but also took a minority interest in her company. Using her expertise and her ability to select only the most valuable opportunities, Krueger has built Cheryl&Co into a successful, multimillion-dollar enterprise.

To explain how people like Krueger discern great opportunities from poor ones, we need to answer three questions:

- How do you select high-leverage opportunities?
- How do you eliminate low-leverage or wasteful activity?
- How do you eliminate the cost of lost opportunity?

Let's look at each of these questions.

How Do You Find and Seize High-Leverage Opportunities?

Krueger knew the difference between a poor opportunity and a great one because of her extensive expertise and her high-leverage thinking. She had learned about purchasing and the art of negotiation as an assistant buyer at Burdine's department store. She had learned retail merchandising and management during four years as merchandising manager at The Limited. She had gained business experience as an assistant vice president with Claus Sportswear.

Thus, with all this experience, before Krueger started her own retail business:

- She had learned how to prove that something would sell, that it could be purchased at the right price and quality, and that it would sell for a profit.
- She had learned how things were made, distributed, promoted, and sold.
- She had learned how to realistically forecast, survey, estimate, and analyze the likely success of an opportunity.

Calculating Benefits Versus Costs

Many see what appears to be a great opportunity for success and then fail when they go after it because they see only the benefits and they underestimate the costs. Krueger says, "What separates a winner from a loser is the ability to be realistic, to do the hard numbers, to be as tough with themselves as a boss would be. And it's easier to be realistic when it's your own money at risk" (from an interview with one of the contributors to this book).

There are many opportunities for success. However, before deciding to seize an opportunity, successful people and successful businesses try to predict how much long-term benefit they would get from it compared with the time, brainpower, and other resources they would have to spend on it.

To select only great opportunities, you must do two things:

- First, you must determine if the opportunity is one of the best opportunities to meet your long-term goals.
- Second, you must calculate the overall value of the opportunity.

The overall value of an opportunity is the expected future benefit of the opportunity minus the costs of seizing it. For example, Krueger expected to create a long-term business that she would love to run and would provide her with lifetime earnings. For that, she was willing to sacrifice a number of years in the beginning, when she put her time and money into the business but had no returns.

To calculate future benefits, risk must be considered. If the opportunity has only a 50-50 chance of success, the expected future benefits are cut in half.

Expected Future Benefits Versus Resources

Even if the opportunity is a very good fit with your long-term goals, and its overall value is high, it may not be the best opportunity in which to invest your resources. Another calculation is needed to find the best opportunity. Figure 4-1 shows that only a portion of opportunities can be pursued with available resources, and thus they should be chosen carefully.

Thinkers like Krueger get an expectation of the return they'll get on the resources they invest by dividing the expected future benefits by the resources required to seize the benefits. The expected future benefits include the increased value and the contribution to long-term strategy, freedom, money, or whatever the seizer considers valuable. Resources include time, money, effort, and whatever is required to seize the benefits.

With regard to short-term versus long-term thinking, many people want short-term payoffs. They won't devote time to preparation, because it doesn't pay off immediately. Because the great achievers knew the long-term value of preparation, they spent their time, thoughts, and resources on activities that had the best combination of short-term and long-term returns.

How Do You Eliminate Wasteful Activity?

The great achievers have known that most activities, events, and transactions in life are wasteful. For instance, Darwin Smith, the CEO of Kimberly-Clark, concluded that

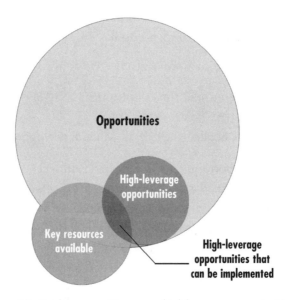

Figure 4-1. Total opportunities versus high-leverage opportunities.

annual forecasts of earnings, a Wall Street tradition, focused too much on the short term and provided no real value to stockholders, so he stopped doing them. He also eliminated titles and management layers before the idea was popular. Under Smith, Kimberly-Clark's stock outperformed those of the other leading paper products companies by four to one. For more on the Kimberly-Clark story, see *Good to Great* by Jim Collins (New York: HarperCollins, 2001).

So, before committing resources to seize an opportunity, the great achievers have made sure that a potential opportunity is the best one to lead them to success. They have all asked several basic questions to increase their chances of success:

- Is this opportunity the largest benefit we can get from our resources?
- Is it worth far more than the time and resources needed to achieve it?
- Can it be done?
- Is it a source of passion for us?

As discussed above, to produce the best results, more resources should be focused on opportunities than on problems. The great achievers have known both where and how to focus resources and where not to focus them. Even when you decide to focus resources on a high-leverage opportunity, you can't do it if wasteful activity fills the day.

Guidelines for Determining if an Activity Is Wasteful

The most important guideline for determining if an activity is wasteful is: It's probably wasteful if you do it routinely without thinking about it—for example, if you do it only because it's

- a problem or a nagging concern
- in your mail, email, or phone messages
- traditional or habitual
- the first solution that pops up
- a policy without regard to its benefits and costs
- a regular meeting
- the popular thing to do
- a solution that always worked in the past.

You've heard people say, "I'm keeping busy." Keeping busy, being active, and "getting things done" pleases many people. However, we should heed the advice of the great basketball coach John Wooden, who said that we must not mistake activity for achievement.

The goal is to pick opportunities that best fit your long-term strategic goals and also have both high, overall value and a high return on your investments of time, brain-power, and resources. Furthermore, as a person gains greater responsibility and influence, he or she should choose opportunities that also have higher overall value.

Although people and organizations don't intentionally waste resources on low-benefit, high-cost activities, they don't always focus on high-leverage opportunities. They naturally drift toward low-leverage ones, which are easier to find, more plentiful, and easier to implement.

Acceptable Opportunities

Here's a test to do before deciding to seize an opportunity: Estimate the lowest reasonable benefits to be expected from the opportunity. Then divide the lowest reasonable benefits by an estimate of the highest reasonable costs to seize the benefits. Most people do the opposite. They calculate the most optimistic benefits with the least cost. The former test is a pessimistic—but safer—approach.

Whether you should take an optimistic or pessimistic approach depends on your level of expertise in the field where you find the opportunity. If you're an expert in this field and can make realistic estimates of benefits and costs, an optimistic approach is appropriate. Risk and available resources also must be considered. The pessimistic test is a guideline instead of a formula to use without judgment.

Small Versus Large Improvements

Although It may seem that this book is focusing primarily on large opportunities, we encourage people to find opportunities to make small improvements as well as large ones. A number of small improvements can add up to big improvements over time. Valuable opportunities for improvement come in all sizes. The smallest opportunity for improvement is valuable if its long-term benefits are greater than the cost of seizing it.

On the one hand, much overall value can be gained from seizing many small opportunities. On the other hand, seizing a few large opportunities or even one great opportunity can produce the same overall value to a person or an organization. The highest-achieving organizations train their people to seize opportunities of all sizes as long as the value of the opportunities is larger than the time, effort, and resources required to seize them.

Every individual in an organization should be trained to focus on activities that produce the best chance for success, because all wasteful activities, no matter how small or how large, use up time and resources that would be better spent on valuable activities. The result is lost opportunity.

How Do You Eliminate the Cost of Lost Opportunity?

When you spend your time, brainpower, and resources on low-leverage activity, you lose the benefits you could have gained if you had spent the time, brainpower, and resources on finding and seizing high-leverage opportunities. This is the cost of lost opportunity. If your organization has competitors, you and your organization fall behind when you lose opportunity.

The Limits of Cost/Benefit Calculations

Every worthwhile activity can't easily be related to long-term benefits. For example, if someone proposes a small improvement that eliminates wasteful activity in an office procedure, it might not go directly to the bottom line. But by encouraging people to make those changes, you develop an organization that is always finding and seizing opportunities. Then, when you're ready to make large improvements, people are more willing.

Earlier in the chapter that discussed Key 2, we pointed out how research shows that when people or organizations are in the process of preparing for, finding, and seizing opportunities for success, they learn at a higher rate and with higher quality. And when they're guided by all 10 keys, they're on the path to success.

How Much Time Should You Invest?

We have been asked if we have discovered a guideline for the percentage of time and activity that individuals and organizations should invest in preparing for, finding, and seizing opportunities. Successful organizations in fast-changing business markets spend at least 20 percent of their total time and activity. Although we don't have exact numbers, the semiconductor and telecommunications industries spend more than that proportion. Startup businesses run as high as 80 percent. The greater the speed of change in your market or the greater amount you must learn in a short time, the greater the share of your time you should spend on finding and seizing opportunities.

Always Search for a Higher Peak

We are on the path of the great achievers if we are preparing for, finding, and seizing the most valuable opportunities, large or small, within our influence. The great achievers searched until they were satisfied that they had found the highest-leverage opportunities within their areas. Like mountain climbers, they searched through the clouds for the highest peaks. We know one top executive who has a method for selecting high-leverage projects. When anyone in her organization proposes that the company invest in a project, she always asks if they could think of any better opportunity. That way, she asks them to always search for a higher peak.

Summary of Keys 1 through 4

To summarize keys 1 through 4:

- First, the great achievers differentiated themselves by choosing to search for opportunity where they had the best chances of finding a great opportunity.
- Second, they became experts through power learning.
- Third, they taught themselves to be exceptional visionaries.
- Fourth, they worked only on opportunities that had the best chances of making them successful compared with the time, brainpower, and resources they had to use to seize them. Figure 4-2 shows how high-leverage knowledge can be applied to pursue high-leverage opportunities. The greater the amount of targeted knowledge, the greater the chances of recognizing and being able to pursue the greatest opportunities.

In the success stories discussed so far, leaders such as Edison, Curie, Walton, Krueger, and Gates knew how to obtain the willing support of others for the projects they chose to make them successful. Our research findings were quite clear on how the great achievers gathered the support of others and why many other opportunity finders stumbled or fell at this point.

Obtaining the Willing Support of Others

The best leaders studied how other great leaders were able to harness the power of others. They discovered three more keys. Guided by these keys, they were able to mobilize the support they needed. The art and science of these keys is the second leg of the path, which makes up part II of this book.

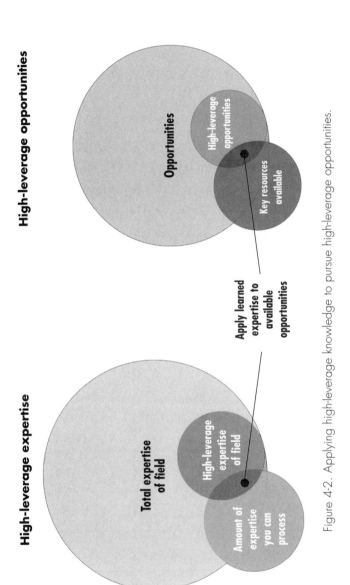

Figure 4-2. Applying high-leverage knowledge to pursue high-leverage opportunities.

Remember that learning is more powerful when you learn in the pursuit of opportunity. So to prepare for the second leg of this learning journey, imagine that you've found a great opportunity for success. However, to seize it, you will need the time and resources of others, who often are less than willing.

 Self-Evaluation Exercises

Select the Best Opportunities for Success

Below, list several opportunities identified from earlier exercises or other opportunities from your business or personal life. First, rate them 1 to 5 in the "return" category, with 5 being the highest potential for expected return. Next, rate them 1 to 5 in the "effort" category, with 5 being the highest effort required.

In the "leverage" (L) column, subtract the effort ranking value (E) from the return ranking value (R) and place the result in the leverage column for each row—as shown in the formula R – E = L. The highest numbers in the leverage column are likely your high-leverage opportunities.

Opportunity	Return	Effort	Leverage
Example — Create personal training business	5	1	4

$$R - E = L$$

Maximizing Your Ability to Pursue High-Leverage Opportunities

Find out how much time you use in pursuing opportunities. Decide what is the most productive part of your day. This is the time when you have the greatest alertness and potential for creativity and focus. You may need to experiment, because it may currently be occupied with other activities that don't require high-leverage thinking. Many people will say they are most productive in early morning, somewhere around the first two hours after waking up. Others may have the most productive potential hours at night after the kids are in bed and when the house is quiet. Dissect an average day to find those two or so optimal hours; use an actual day, if possible. List the amount of time consumed by each activity, give a description of the activity, and place a check next to the category to the right that best describes it.

	Time	Activity	Search for and implement opportunity	Communication	Meeting	Routine business or personal maintenance activities	Other routine business or personal activities	Other activities
Example	8–8:30 am	Read and respond to email		✓				

Compare the activities listed above with the opportunities listed in the previous exercise. For most, these precious, high-productivity potential hours of the day are used for activities other than pursuing high-leverage opportunities. Discover how you could rearrange your schedule so that you can use this productive part of the day for creative preparation, finding or seizing activities to support your opportunities.

Part II

Mobilize Support

*Visions are never the sole property of one man or one woman.
Before a vision can become reality, it must be owned
by every single member of the group.*

—Phil Jackson, winner of nine NBA titles

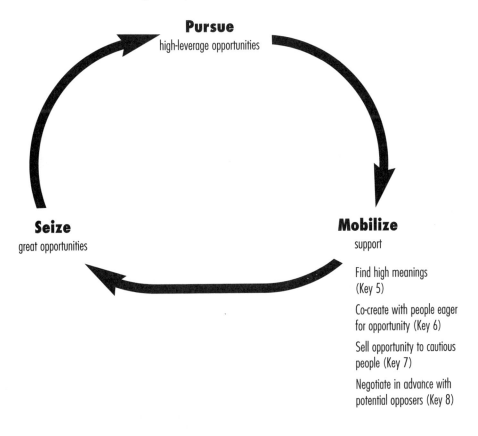

Pursue
high-leverage opportunities

Mobilize
support

Find high meanings
(Key 5)

Co-create with people eager
for opportunity (Key 6)

Sell opportunity to cautious
people (Key 7)

Negotiate in advance with
potential opposers (Key 8)

Seize
great opportunities

ave you imagined that you found a great opportunity for success that you needed the help of others to seize? All the great achievers needed the help of others to succeed. Edison was always searching for financial investors for his projects. Michelangelo sought and received the patronage of many powerful people, including Lorenzo and Giuliano de' Medici and Pope Julius II.

Although Bill Gates has outstanding technical aptitude, his ability to influence others to support his ventures has made him the leader of the personal computer software revolution and the richest person in the world. By convincing IBM to buy nonexclusive rights to the operating system he developed for its personal computer, he was able to legally sell the same software to all the companies that cloned IBM's personal computer.

The most successful people and organizations were guided by keys 5 through 8, shown in the diagram on the previous page. In this way, they multiplied themselves through others. To mobilize support, you need to identify what has great value or meaning to those from whom you wish to gain support.

Key 5

Find High Meanings

In exploring key 5, we need to know the answer to four questions:

- How do we gain the respect of others?
- How do we begin to involve others?
- How do we see opportunity from others' eyes?
- How do we find the high meanings that will inspire others to change?

Let's look at each of these questions.

How Do We Gain the Respect of Others?

When the great achievers didn't respect the power of others, they paid a dear price—as in the case of the next visionary. His story begins in a courtroom years ago, as he was ushered in.

The Trial

A bearded old man, he walked unsteadily, his deep-set eyes piercing the room. He was fearful. In his 70 years, he had never been on trial before. His doctors had told the court that he would die if removed from his sickbed, but the court had ordered him to appear anyway.

The prosecutor, a thin, heavily wrinkled man, robed in red and purple, was seated at a small oak table. For him, this was a must-win trial. Far more was at stake than the crime; both the law and the system were on trial. The defendant had to be stopped. The prosecutor rose and, without facing the defendant, began his examination: "Do you have anything to say?"

The old man sighed deeply. "I have nothing to say." In contrast to his thin, clean-shaven opponents, the old man was a large, swarthy man with an immense beard and a bald head that stretched far behind a deeply furrowed forehead (figure 5-1).

The prosecutor narrowed his eyes as he turned toward the old man. "Do you hold or have you held that the sun, not the earth, is the center of the universe?"

The defendant knew what he had to say to save his life: "I hold the opinion the earth is the center of the universe."

His thoughts drifted back to the beginning. It began when he built a telescope so powerful that he could see ships 50 miles out on the Aegean Sea. When he invited members of the Venetian Senate to look through his telescope, they were amazed. Overnight, the military and commercial world fell at his feet.

The prosecutor scowled. He lifted a copy of the old man's book, *Dialogue*, from the table. "Do you hold the opinion the earth goes around the sun?" He slammed the book to the table. "Tell the truth!"

"I did not write the book because I hold that opinion," the old man replied.

"I repeat. From the nature of the book, you have held the opinion the earth moves about the sun." The prosecutor's voice rose to a shout. "Tell the truth! Otherwise, we will torture!"

The old man slumped in his chair. He knew that, a few years earlier, a Franciscan friar, Giordano Bruno, had been brutally tortured and then burned alive for heretical beliefs.

Figure 5-1. An illustration of Galileo before the Inquisition (© Corbis)

"I am here to obey," he said, with what appeared to be all his remaining strength.

The old man's thoughts drifted again. If only he'd been content to view ships at sea. But he had improved his telescope until he could see what no one had ever seen: moons rotating around other planets. He remembered being frozen to the eyepiece. What he saw contradicted Aristotle's theory that all heavenly bodies rotated around the Earth.

The long silence in the courtroom ended when the prosecutor returned from his huddle with the inquisitor. He said that the trial was over. The old man was led back to his cell.

The next day, he knelt before his inquisitors and said in a weak voice, "I, Galileo Galilei . . . swear that I've always believed, I believe now, and, with God's help, will always believe all that is held and preached by the Holy Catholic Church."

Galileo was sentenced to house arrest for life and barred from ever expressing his views. He had to publicly apologize. His book was forbidden, and his condemnation read to professors and students of science in Italy.

He was angry. Why had they done this to him? With his telescope, he had shown them that Jupiter had four moons circling it. He was sure that they'd marvel at the power of the Creator. But they refused to "see." Eight years later, he died a prisoner in his villa in Arcetri, just outside Florence. For more on this story, see the source for this synopsis: *Galileo* by James Reston Jr. (New York: HarperCollins, 1994).

For centuries, people have debated whether Galileo got a fair trial. There are good arguments on both sides. Put yourself in the church's position. Suppose you believed that the splendor you saw above you on a dark night was heaven. Galileo was asking you to believe that you were seeing just more suns and planets. If Galileo were right, the Earth would be revolving at 1,000 miles an hour, and we'd be orbiting the sun at 67,000 miles an hour. The winds would blow us over, and we'd be flung off. A ball thrown into the air would not fall straight down. But we're not flung off, the winds don't blow us over, and a ball does fall straight down. It's obvious that we're standing still and that the heavens revolve about us.

Of course that view is wrong, but you'll never be able to lead where others can't lead until you learn to respect the expertise of those who have different views of the world. We're not saying that you should condone the view of the church at that time. But you can respect and appreciate it. In his book, Galileo made fools of those who believed that the Earth was the center of the universe. These included the Pope. A leader must have more than the truth; he must know how to help others see it. When some visionaries become frustrated with those who oppose or resist their vision, they attack them. They make war and they get war; there's a winner, there's a loser. And when they underestimate the relative power of the resisters, they're the losers.

Of course ideas like Galileo's are always going to elicit opposition. The theory of evolution that Charles Darwin proposed was also highly controversial. But Darwin welcomed the challenges of others and openly questioned his own work. Darwin respected the power, expertise, and viewpoints of others. He, in turn, was so respected that many colleagues who disagreed with him did not attack him.

The Lesson of the Stone

The type of marble that Michelangelo sculpted *David* from is pure white marble, the finest in the world. It has been mined in the Alpi Alpuan Mountains near Carrara, Italy, since the time of the Roman Empire. This marble has the least impurities of all marble, but even it will shatter if struck in the wrong place. It's unforgiving. The stone will not forgive a lack of expertise in carving. One wrong blow from the hammer and the stone will shatter and the sculpture will be ruined. The sculptor must not only expertly visualize the final image inside the stone but must also know where to strike the stone so it will willingly yield the final image.

Michelangelo knew the lesson of the stone. His mother died when he was a baby, and he was sent to the wife of a stonecutter to be wet-nursed. All his life, Michelangelo remembered the reverence of the old stonecutters toward the stone and their mystical words of caution: "The power lay in the stone, not in the arms or the tools. If ever a mason came to think he was master, the stone would oppose him." For more on Michelangelo, see *The Agony and the Ecstasy* by Irving Stone (New York: Signet, 1961).

Great leaders know the lesson of the stone. They approach each new mission with the humility of a sculptor. They know that if they put themselves above people, people will oppose them.

As we studied great failures, such as Galileo's, we found that leaders often failed when they thought they were superior—when they didn't respect the expertise and power of those who opposed them. In the mid–eighteenth century, the king of England imposed stiff new taxes and laws on the American colonies without their consent. He thought they had no choice but to comply. You know the rest of the story.

Great leaders mobilize support by first respecting the expertise and power of others.

How Do We Begin to Involve Others?

Leaders who don't see opportunity from the eyes of others make many common errors: The first error is to fail to identify and involve others early enough in the process. The second error is to not know or care about the needs and wants of others—as Galileo did. The third is to overestimate the acceptance of others, and the fourth is to underestimate the power of the opposition. To avoid common leadership errors:

- Identify and involve others early.
- Know the needs and wants of others.
- Don't overestimate the acceptance of others.
- Don't underestimate the power of the opposition.

Let's discuss each of these briefly.

Identify and Involve Others Early

To identify whom to involve, a leader must imagine what the future will be like once the opportunity is seized. Two groups of people must be identified: those whose help is needed to seize the opportunity, and those whose lives will be changed by seizing the opportunity. Here's a checklist for identifying those who must be involved:

- Who stands to gain the most from seizing this opportunity?
- Whose time, expertise, and resources are needed to seize the opportunity?
- Who are the power insiders that must be involved to seize the opportunity?
- Who needs to change what they are doing to seize the opportunity?
- Which employees, customers, or suppliers will be affected significantly?
- Who will oppose seizing the opportunity?

Know the Needs and Wants of Others

Even the great achievers sometimes lose sight of the needs and wants of others. Early in the 20th century, Henry Ford's ability to see that his customers wanted an affordable, durable automobile made him a giant in the automobile industry. But, in 1925, General Motors introduced car buyers to variety, style, yearly model changes, and financing. At that time, Ford had lost touch with the needs and wants of his most important customers. He continued to build only one model and denounced financing as evil. By 1927, his firm had lost most of its customers. After suffering huge losses and being threatened with ruin, Ford changed his mind and provided variety, model changes, and financing.

Winning customers back was costly for Henry Ford. Research has shown that it's much more expensive to win a new customer than it is to keep an existing one. So it's important to know your customer's real wants and needs.

Certainly, there are times when a leader must do what's right, no matter what others may think they need. However, a leader will get less opposition if he or she explains the reasons for unpopular changes, because this shows people that the leader respects their needs. People still may not like it, but many will understand that it's necessary for the long-term benefit of them and the organization.

Don't Overestimate the Acceptance of Others, and Don't Underestimate the Power of the Opposition

The most successful people are energized by the visions they create and are stimulated by change. On the one hand, these are great strengths. On the other hand, they're sometimes so passionate that they can't see a vision through the eyes of those affected by the vision. See the sidebar for how Abraham Lincoln made this mistake.

Some leaders leave the opposition out until they are sure they can seize the opportunity. All may go well in the beginning, but when the opposition hears about it, they feel left out, and the leaders lose their trust. The opposers then exaggerate rumors of changes and job cuts or whatever is at stake. Then the leaders have a battle on their hands.

Abraham Lincoln was a master of human relations. But during the Civil War, he had an ex-member of Congress, Clement Vallandigham, jailed after an antiwar speech and he revoked the writ of habeas corpus so that all critics of the war could be jailed indefinitely. He then shut down the *Chicago Times* because of its antiwar views. All over the nation, speakers rose to condemn the arrests, the war, and an unjust draft that allowed the rich to hire people to take their places. In New York City, police and marines couldn't stop the mobs when they rioted against the draft. Hundreds were killed.

Lincoln's staunchest supporters pleaded with him to back off. Lincoln, surprised by the reaction, freed the critics, allowed the *Times* to publish again, and reinstated the writ of habeas corpus. Even a great leader like Lincoln sometimes overestimated the acceptance of others.

Visionaries know that there is great opportunity above because they see it from below. Or, having been to the top, they know that the journey is worth it. But others may see just a few steps ahead. In general, it is a mistake to assume that others will follow. Great leaders know that others are more willing to follow when they "see" what is at the top and find personal meaning in climbing to reach it.

The best leaders identify those who should be involved early. Then, to get them to willingly invest their time, expertise, and resources, the best leaders try to see the opportunity from their point of view.

There may be no one who is better able to "see what others see" than the next master.

How Do We See Opportunity Through Others' Eyes?

In 1976, the WJZ-TV newsroom in Baltimore received a call from a reporter at the scene of a fire. The reporter said that the station should not do a story on the fire because it was too horrifying. The news desk ordered her to cover it. Obediently, she interviewed a woman who had lost seven children in the fire. She cried with the woman as the camera rolled.

That evening, after the film was aired, the reporter apologized on the air for crying. Co-workers criticized her for her loss of control and considered her apology unprofessional. She was told that she didn't have the "right stuff" for big-city reporting. The station gave her a second chance as a news co-anchor but quickly removed her.

Then a new manager decided to create a morning talk show to run opposite the popular Phil Donohue show. The ex-reporter was selected as a co-host. Most believed that the show had a slim chance of success, but the ex-reporter had something the odds-makers didn't know about. She was a genius at finding the human-interest side of a guest's story and asking questions that the audience wanted to ask. She won the respect of guests because she gave them respect and was genuinely interested in them. For example, guests knew that if they had been abused or unsuccessful with dieting, she understood. Soon, all Baltimore was talking about her, and the show ratings climbed. She said to herself, "This is what I should be doing. It's like breathing."

Of course, we're talking about Oprah Winfrey. Oprah had found a career she had a passion for, one in which her apparent weakness—her ability to see from others' points of view—was valuable human expertise. For more on this story, see the source of the material above: *The Uncommon Wisdom of Oprah Winfrey* by Bill Adler (New York: Carol Publishing, 1997).

These days, *The Oprah Winfrey Show* is seen by 20 million viewers a week. People invest hundreds of millions of dollars in the products she supports. Oprah used her leadership and business expertise to build a billion-dollar business. She has a lesson to teach all of us: When we learn to see from others' points of view, we show our respect for them and we gain their respect.

The Customer's Point of View

Intuit Corporation, the maker of popular personal and small-business accounting software, continually searches for what existing customers "see." All Intuit employees, including the CEO, are required periodically to staff the customer service telephones and respond to and solve customers' problems. Customer thank-you letters are posted on the company's walls for all to see. At company meetings, the first items on the agenda are customer service trends, problems, and victories. This tells the employees what the customers "see" and what the employees are doing to please the customers. For more on this approach, see *Extreme Management* by Mark Stevens (New York: Warner Business Books, 2001).

Seeing from the customer's point of view has created breakthrough marketing approaches. See the sidebar for examples.

The Employee's Point of View

Finding what it takes to energize employees to give more than what the job requires is an important leadership function. Employees may want more training or

---

Dozens of patents were awarded for safety razors around the turn of the 20th century. Among them was one by King Gillette. His razor was different from, but not superior to, many of the others. It cost a dollar to produce his razor—more than he could sell one for. But Gillette figured out the shaver's point of view. The shaver would buy his razor if it were priced at 55 cents, well below the competitors' prices. After that, the shaver would willingly pay 5 cents each for the blades. As a blade cost less than 1 cent to make, Gillette could afford a big loss on the razor while making a profit on sales of blades. He made money on the shave, not on the razor. Xerox did a similar thing by placing expensive copiers in offices and charging 5 cents a copy. These and other stories are related by Peter F. Drucker in *The Essential Drucker* (New York: Harper Business, 2001).

---

increased responsibility in their jobs. They may want to have a say in how the work is done. They may want to be part of a mission with a high purpose. They may want more job security. It is important to see the world from their points of view.

How Do We Find the High Meanings That Will Inspire Others to Change?

Great leaders search for the high meaning that will inspire others to give their minds and hearts. In 1940, personal survival was on every British citizen's mind. At that time, Great Britain stood alone in Europe against a mighty German war machine that had swept through Poland, Czechoslovakia, and France. It was clear that Hitler would soon attack the British homeland. As concerned British citizens huddled around the radio, the prime minister, Winston Churchill, spoke in the clipped and inspiring tones he was famous for:

> HITLER KNOWS HE WILL HAVE TO BREAK US ON THIS ISLAND OR LOSE THE WAR. IF WE CAN STAND UP TO HIM, ALL EUROPE WILL BE FREE, AND THE LIFE OF THE WORLD MAY MOVE FORWARD INTO BROAD, SUNLIT UPLANDS. BUT IF WE FAIL, THE WHOLE WORLD, INCLUDING THE UNITED STATES, INCLUDING ALL WE HAVE KNOWN AND CARED FOR, WILL SINK INTO THE ABYSS OF A NEW DARK AGE. . . . LET US THERE-FORE BRACE OURSELVES TO OUR DUTIES AND SO BEAR OURSELVES THAT IF THE BRITISH EMPIRE AND ITS COMMONWEALTH LAST FOR A THOUSAND YEARS, MEN WILL SAY, THIS WAS OUR FINEST HOUR.

Churchill's speech roused the spirit of the people, elevating them above their fear, above their self-interest. In the darkest hour of the 20th century, he stood like a shining light. He knew what influenced human action. The quotation above is from *The Penguin Book of Historic Speeches*, edited by Brian MacArthur (New York: Penguin Books, 1996). The context in which the speech was given is from *Churchill: A Life* by Martin Gilbert (New York: Henry Holt, 1991).

There are many theories about what influences our actions. Some of the most respected theories are:

- Meanings are programmed in us for survival and adaptation.
- Our culture greatly influences our adaptive behavior.
- There is a hierarchy of human needs.
- We all have a need for meaning.

Let's look at each of these basic theories.

Meanings Are Programmed in Us for Survival and Adaptation

Some anthropologists theorize that humans are programmed to survive and adapt by rewarding two opposite behaviors: caution and adventure. It's as if we are pulled in two opposite directions:

- The *adventurous pull* rewards us for exploring, risk taking, discovering, pushing our limits, and fighting.
- The *cautious pull* rewards us when we rest our minds and bodies, conserve our energy and resources, preserve ourselves, and flee from danger.

One opportunity may have very different meanings for different people. The cautious individual may see danger in the opportunity, while the adventurous individual sees excitement and rewards. Most leaders are on the adventurous side, and they often are impatient with those on the cautious side. They prod others to explore, to take risks, to set unimaginable goals, and to make changes.

Our Culture Greatly Influences Our Adaptive Behavior

The Chinese were the first to make paper, to make silk, to use block letters to print, to invent gunpowder, to create the first water-driven machine for the spinning of hemp, and to use coal and coke in blast furnaces. Although they found all these opportunities, the opportunities all were seized and turned into huge enterprises by the Europeans.

In *Why Are Some So Rich and Others So Poor?* (New York: W. W. Norton, 1998), the researcher David S. Landes says that not only did the ancient Chinese lack free markets and property rights, they didn't seize these opportunities because they valued tradition, and the leaders wanted to keep the power in their hands. They were cautious, whereas the Europeans were adventuresome. The Chinese culture today is becoming more adventuresome and more successful.

There Is a Hierarchy of Human Needs

Another popular theory is the psychologist Abraham Maslow's hierarchy of needs; see his *Maslow on Management* (New York: Wiley, 1988). According to Maslow, basic needs at the bottom of the hierarchy must be satisfied before higher needs become important. Maslow said that whatever needs a person is experiencing affect the person's motivations, priorities, and behaviors. Unsatisfied needs create the motivation to satisfy them. People need to satisfy the needs at each lower level—at least partially—before they can move on to a higher level, ultimately self-actualization. Together, these needs form a pyramid (figure 5-2).

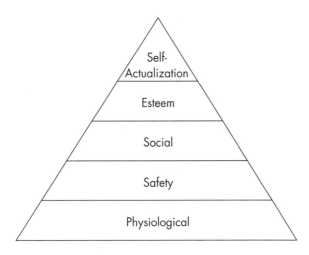

Figure 5-2. Abraham Maslow's hierarchy of needs.

Many people in industrial countries today are not focusing on mere survival. Thus, they can focus on creating new products and developing themselves. In the more advanced countries, each year, more work requires innovation, and those who can innovate are functioning higher on Maslow's pyramid. Leaders in advanced countries who help people move toward the top of the pyramid will get them to give more than what is required.

Some behaviorists say that the higher the purpose, the higher the meaning. People do volunteer work partly because they believe in what they're doing. If they are asked to do work that they don't enjoy doing for a good cause or a higher purpose, many would probably do it, even though that wouldn't necessarily be the best use of their expertise. Others might resist. It isn't enough for an organization to have a high purpose to get people to dedicate themselves to its mission. The best volunteer organizations we studied discover a volunteer's expertise and place the volunteer in a job where the person will be challenged to use that expertise to the fullest. Many volunteers were more enthusiastic about their unpaid work than about what they did for a living.

The more freedom of choice and opportunities people have, the more they must work to find ways to make their willing contribution to achieving the mission. The most progressive of today's leaders treat all people they lead as if they're volunteers.

As the amount of available knowledge increases rapidly, businesses must acquire knowledge more rapidly and more effectively to remain competitive. This means that a worker's knowledge and ability to use it are vital resources. Therefore, knowledgeable people have to be managed as if they were volunteers.

We All Have a Need for Meaning

Another relevant theory is about humanity's need for meaning. Meanings are powerful beams of light in the worst darkness. In *Man's Search for Meaning* (Boston: Beacon Press, 1984), Viktor Frankl, who survived German concentration camps, says that those who survived had meaning that made the brutal conditions tolerable. Some felt that they needed to take care of loved ones or that they still had unfinished work. Others felt that surviving was a way of winning against their hated captors. Frankl proposed that the highest meanings are those for which people will endure any difficulty and choose to survive when death would be easier. He believed that meaning is the best motivator for development, improvement, and change. The meaning that something or someone has for us includes:

- the value, moral or psychological significance, need, or importance to us
- what we stand to lose by its or the person's absence
- what we stand to gain by acquiring it or having the person in our lives.

In general, no matter what theory of human behavior they were inclined to believe, the great leaders always searched for higher meanings when they were trying to influence others to change.

Converting People Into Investors

Our research team found that great leaders influenced others in a way we couldn't put into words. Traditional words, such as ownership, participation, and involvement, didn't describe how they led. Then one of our researchers suggested that great leaders convert people into investors.

Initially, no one agreed with her. But she said that the team members were thinking too narrowly about the word "investor." She asked them to think of broader definitions of invest, such as "devote time or provide ideas to a purpose" or "contribute effort to something in the hope of future benefit." For example, if someone on your staff willingly proposes a better way to do a job, she's an investor. However, if she thinks you won't listen to her, or that she'll lose if her idea fails, she may not invest. If one of your engineers willingly works unpaid over a weekend to test a new product, he's an investor. The time you willingly give your children is an investment.

Our researcher said that thinking of people as potential investors of their time, ideas, and resources greatly improves how we approach them for their help. In time, we all agreed that converting people into investors is the best way to describe what great leaders did to mobilize people to seize opportunities. We decided that, from that point on, we would define an investor as "any person or group that willingly gives time, ideas, or resources to seize an opportunity, in the hope of future benefit."

So, to mobilize support, we should first identify those who should be involved and then learn what meanings influence their behaviors. We are then prepared to convert them into investors with the help of the next three keys: co-creating with the eager ones, selling the cautious ones, and negotiating with potential opposers. It's important to be skilled in the use of these keys. It's also important to know which key will be most effective with each group.

Willingness to Invest

When an opportunity for success is first introduced, people's willingness to invest varies widely. As shown in phase I on the left side of figure 5-3, people can be divided into three groups, according to their willingness to invest and what has the most meaning for them.

These three groups can be described this way:

- A small group of people, the *eager investors*—sometimes called *early adopters* or *pioneers*—is looking for opportunity and is willing to change. Seizing the opportunity has high meaning for them.

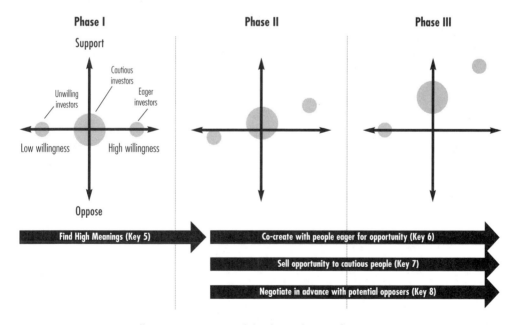

Figure 5-3. Willingness to invest and the three phases of seizing an opportunity.

- A much larger group, the *cautious investors*, wants to keep things the way they are, because keeping things the way they are has high meaning for them. Many of them are pragmatic, however, and can be sold on the opportunity.
- Another small group, the *unwilling investors*, initially may oppose the opportunity, either because the individuals believe that the opportunity is against their interests or because they're championing other opportunities that compete for the same resources. Blocking the opportunity has high meaning for them.

Figure 5-3 shows the three typical phases of how you can seize an opportunity. In phase I, you apply key 5 to identify investors and what meanings influence their behavior. You search for their higher meanings.

In phase II, you apply keys 6, 7, and 8 to gain support from eager and cautious investors while keeping potential opposition from unwilling investors in check. Note that the leftmost circle, which represents unwilling investors, moves down and becomes an opposing force. This is the typical reaction from this group, and only continued use of good technique can bring them up to a more neutral position.

Phase III shows that the proper implementation of keys 6, 7, and 8 will typically result in a distribution where maximum support is achieved from eager investors, strong support is achieved from cautious investors, and the opposition from unwilling investors is mostly neutralized.

These techniques, as outlined in figure 5-3, are covered in detail in keys 6, 7, and 8. In key 6, we'll first consider how to best get the willing support of eager investors.

Self-Evaluation Exercise: Maximize Support for Pursuit of Opportunity

List the key people most important to your business or personal goals and opportunities in the left-hand column below. Check the boxes that most accurately reflect how you interact with them.

Key contributors	Co-create with them	Discuss strategy and mission goals with them	Involve them early on new ventures	Respect their expertise	Respect their viewpoint	Search for and understand what their highest meanings are
Example Bob Willard	✓			✓		

Look for any opportunities in the above list to create investors and volunteers from your key contributors.

Key 6

Co-Create with People Eager for Opportunity

People support what they create.

—Kurt Lewin

Great leaders have the answer to the question: How do we influence those who are most eager to invest? They are often those who eagerly seek opportunity, have high motivation to create change, and will influence others.

How Do We Influence Those Most Eager to Invest?

The next great innovator's ability to influence those most eager to invest was critical to his seizing a great opportunity. His story begins at the moment he faced bankruptcy.

After months of preparation, in early 1973, Fred Smith, his wife, and his office staff stood at the end of a runway on a small airfield in Memphis, Tennessee. They were waiting for six small jets to arrive with packages to be delivered overnight. A makeshift con-veyor and sorting table were set up in an old hangar, and employees were standing by. Everyone knew that this was the last chance. All day, reports from sales agents had been optimistic, and Smith was ready to celebrate. Just before midnight, six tiny lights appeared in the sky. After the jets landed and roared to a stop, everyone moved toward them. When the doors of the first plane were opened, the group looked into the cargo hold to see the contents.

Empty! They looked into the other planes; there were only five paid packages. The group couldn't believe it. Smith was shocked. Surely now, his family, financial backers, friends, and staff believed, he would come to his senses, give up overnight package delivery, and do something else for a living. Three strikes in the overnight delivery business and you're out.

Smith's first attempt to make overnight deliveries was carrying securities for bond houses. But when insurers wouldn't guarantee those shipments, his business fizzled. Then he decided to fly checks between Federal Reserve branch banks. The Federal Reserve branches encouraged him because they could envision big savings. But by the time he had bought two airplanes, named his company Federal Express (FedEx), and was ready with a working system, the Federal Reserve had scrapped the idea.

Then Smith came up with the idea of overnight package delivery. His company would pick up packages, fly them to Memphis and sort them, and then deliver them to their destinations the next morning. Fred chose six cities close to Memphis for his trial run. He bought four more planes, expanded his crew, and hired a salesforce. The result was those six planes with only the five paid packages.

On the edge of bankruptcy, Smith asked his team members to stick with the business and to invest their time to help him create a successful overnight delivery business. They agreed. After two weeks of 16-hours-a-day analysis, the team members decided they had chosen the wrong cities to start with. They had chosen cities a short flight from Memphis rather than cities that needed the air freight service. For example, they'd picked New Orleans, which had a weak industrial base and was well serviced by Delta Airlines. So they searched for cities with strong industries but poor air service—like Rochester, New York, the home of Kodak and Xerox—that most needed overnight delivery.

In April, Smith and his team gathered again at midnight at the airport and waited for the planes to return from the newly selected destinations. They all agreed that they had given it their best shot. If it didn't work this time, they were through. After the planes rolled to a stop, the group quietly approached. When the first plane's cargo doors were opened, they again pressed to look into the hold. They were surprised and elated; the planes were filled with hundreds of packages. The team's plan had worked, and they now were committed, for better or worse.

Shortly afterward, it did get worse. In one crisis, while juggling his cash to keep the company afloat, Smith issued a memo with all employees' paychecks, stating that they were welcome to cash their checks but that it would be helpful if some of them waited a few days. Almost everyone waited. Some employees never cashed those checks. Many of them proudly have the framed checks hanging on their office walls.

Smith's team continued to fight its way through obstacles until FedEx was delivering thousands of packages each day. It was the fastest company in history to reach $1 billion in sales. Today, FedEx delivers 2.5 million packages a day and is a $24 billion enterprise, according to its 2004 annual report.

Great leaders like Fred Smith know how to influence those who are eager for opportunity, those who are often called "early adopters." When those eager for opportunity are willing to invest, they'll influence others to invest. In figure 6-1, the darkest shaded circle at the top right represents the results of properly co-creating with these eager investors—who have the most potential of the three investor groups to become great supporters. The effective use of the techniques described here usually moves this group up toward support, as the two other circles in the figure show.

Co-Creation

Effective leaders like Fred Smith work with those who are eager for opportunity to jointly create the opportunity, so they are willing to invest in seizing it. We call this co-creation. Co-creation works because, as Kurt Lewin said, "People support what they create." And everyone has something creative to contribute, which leads to a first law of meaning.

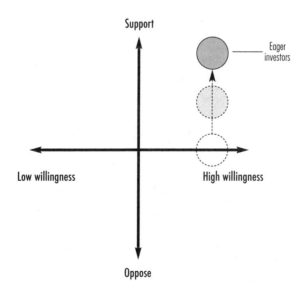

Figure 6-1. Eager investors and willingness to invest.

The First Law of Meaning: People support what they create. Co-creation is a timeless key. In A.D. 100, Columella, a Roman landlord, wrote about managing his workforce: "Nowadays, I make it a practice to call them into consultation on any new work. I observe they're more willing to set about a piece of work when their opinions are asked and their advice followed."

Centuries later, the genius inventor Thomas Edison co-created with his team. A machinist who worked for Edison for 50 years said, "He made me feel I was making something with him; not just a workman."

By building environments that favor co-creation, organizations increase their chances that eager investors will step forward and invest their time and ideas. For example, in the late 1980s, NASA asked Lockheed Martin to cut the weight of the huge fuel tank that forms the backbone of the space shuttle. An engineering team used stronger, lighter-weight materials to reduce the weight but fell 800 pounds short of the target. However, the team had widely dispersed the knowledge of the weight-cut target to the workforce. One line worker knew that 200 gallons of paint was being used to paint the tank, and he knew that a gallon weighed about 4 pounds, amounting to a total weight of 800 pounds. He also knew the tank had a 10-minute lifespan before it was jettisoned. He suggested that they stop painting the tank. The engineers listened, and NASA agreed. The line worker invested his idea in the effort because the Lockheed Martin managers were open to co-creation.

Few leaders are better at co-creation than Norman Bodek, the founder of Productivity Inc. and the acknowledged founding father in this country of the "lean" movement, which follows a system of principles to eliminate waste and generally do more with less. These principles are built on Toyota's production system and the lessons it learned from U.S. auto manufacturers in the 1950s. "Lean," thus, usually refers to highly productive business systems that are customer focused, with low inventory, quick turnaround, and few defects.

In the early 1980s, Bodek introduced American business to these very productive lean methods. He believes that every person has the capacity and desire to be a problem solver and to be a source of creative ideas. His mission was once suggested in a Chinese fortune cookie: "You have the talent to recognize the talent in others."

With many great successes to his credit, Bodek now spends his time teaching managers how to help people use their creative abilities. He founded the publishing company PCS Press to spread his message. "I see myself," he says, "as the Johnny Appleseed of empowering people to believe in themselves and their creative abilities."

Toward Key 7

We're now ready for the great achievers' key 7. To prepare for this key, recall the times you have seen leaders fail, even though they have the willing support of "eager investors."

Even adventuresome people have difficulty changing what's been good to them for many years. Even when logic says "change or else" or when the situation is highly uncomfortable, they may hold on to the way things are. Either they have a lot invested in the way things are or they've experienced too much change lately. Or maybe they don't mind change but they mind being changed. Most people are not easily changed; they are cautious and pragmatic. Let's examine why they're cautious.

Key 7

Sell Opportunity
to Cautious People

You must change people's minds. And you can't just root out a handful of complex ideas and leave a void behind—you have to give people something that is as meaningful as what they've lost!

—Daniel Quinn, *Ishmael*

Over the years, the medical field has been cautious—for good reason. However, one of the most important medical breakthroughs in history was made because an eager surgeon was influenced by a great scientist to seize an opportunity. At the time, doctors ridiculed a new idea that tiny germs could kill a large animal or a human. They believed that germs spontaneously appeared and that people either inherited their susceptibility to them or succumbed because they were being punished for evildoing. Then a French scientist, Louis Pasteur, discovered that germs could kill large animals and that germs came from other diseased persons or animals. However, as late as 1872, a professor at the University of Toulouse said that Pasteur's germ theory was a ridiculous fiction. Pasteur infuriated doctors by saying that 50 percent of all surgery patients died because they were infected during surgery. He proposed that surgeons disinfect themselves, their instruments, and the area of the patient that was open during surgery. Influenced by Pasteur's writings, a surgeon named Joseph Lister developed antiseptic methods that reduced the death rate from his surgeries from nearly 50 percent to 12 percent. Others followed Lister. In the next 10 years, thousands of surgeons adopted his methods.

Almost all major innovations in history were spread only after some eager investor produced results so impressive that some of the cautious ones became willing to try the idea.

The Concerns of the Cautious

People are cautious for good reason. Their caution often is expressed in the personal and business questions they ask when they are asked to make changes. The personal questions are:

- Why should we change? Why now? Why us? Why me?
- What if I make a mistake? Will I be worse off after the change?
- What will my new job be? What will the new organization look like?
- How and when will the change be made?
- Does the organization care about what happens to me?
- Will I have a say in what happens, or will they ignore what I think?
- Will I have a role or position as good as the one I have today?
- Will my expertise be as needed and as valuable?
- Will I lose power or influence? Whom will I work for? Will I have a job at all?
- If I lose my job, how will I support my family?
- Where will I find another job?

The business questions and considerations are:

- Is the technology proven?
- Is this opportunity real and long term, or is it just another wild idea or passing fad?
- Is there a clear, low-risk return on any investment we might make?
- Who else in my market has done this? Were they successful?
- We already have our plates full; where would we get the resources?
- Why can't we wait until the opportunity is more widely tried and proven successful?
- Will my boss or the rest of the organization buy into it?
- What is the hidden downside to the perceived opportunity?
- Is there a safe exit strategy if it doesn't work?

As related in his book *The Diffusion of Innovations* (New York: Free Press, 1995), the researcher Everett Rogers found five factors that determine how fast innovations are adopted within a culture:

- the relative advantage of the new method or technology
- the compatibility of the new method or technology with adopters' existing beliefs and customs

- how simple and easy it is to use
- how easily it can be tried or experienced
- how observable the results are.

Note that all five factors are viewed from the eyes of the potential adopter.

Many cautious people want to keep things the way they are—not only because the way things are has high meaning for them but also because they would rather wait until the opportunity has been proved before they invest. This is the large group shown in the middle of figure 7-1. If selling techniques are used effectively, this group moves up to a supporting role, as the figure shows.

To get this large group to invest, you must be able to answer this question: How do we influence those who have high meaning with their present states—who are skeptical, who don't like change, or who are weary of change?

How Do We Influence Those Who Are Skeptical, Pragmatic, or Resistant to Change?

High achievers have high meaning with the present state and often are the most cautious of all investors.

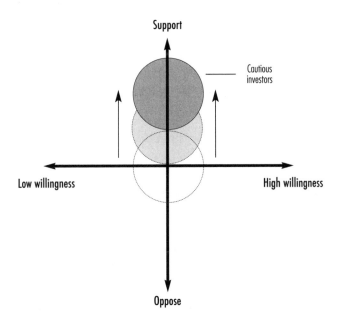

Figure 7-1. Cautious investors and willingness to invest.

Influencing High Achievers

Those who have found an area of work in which they have high expertise, high passion, and are well rewarded have often found and seized great opportunities that have made them highly successful. So when they see that a new opportunity is in a field or area of work where they have less expertise, where they have less passion, or where the rewards may be less, they may be cautious about change. The sidebar gives an example of how this caution shook one company and its people to their foundations.

Cautious resistance like Motorola's, even when an organization or individual is aware of widespread change such as that to digital phone technology, is called the paradox of differentiation.

The Differentiation Paradox

Differentiating yourself and/or your organization for opportunity is essential to finding great opportunities. Yet that same differentiation can keep you from finding opportunities in a market or an industry that has changed greatly. For example:

- A small retailer may be faced with a Wal-Mart down the street that offers the same products at 30 percent less.
- A wholesale distribution business may be faced with a major retailer, such as Wal-Mart, that is buying directly from factories in China.
- A manager in a manufacturing plant must learn lean manufacturing methods or lose business to a manufacturer in South Korea.

When world markets change rapidly, how you have differentiated your organization for opportunity—that is, the work for which you have high expertise and high passion—may no longer be well rewarded.

In the late 1980s, Motorola was the dominant player in the mobile telephone business, with a world market share of 35 percent. In the 1990s, Nokia, an upstart in the mobile phone business, began to offer phones with digital technology, which became the European standard. As Nokia's market share grew steadily, Motorola was cautious and resisted moving into the digital phone business. In fact, Motorola increased its investment and effort in analog mobile phones. By the end of 2000, Nokia's world market share had increased to 35 percent and Motorola's had dropped to 15 percent. Does it seem strange that Motorola saw the rewards shifting to digital mobile phone makers yet resisted moving in that direction?

So this is the paradox: The way you differentiated yourself was the key to your success, but now it keeps you from finding and seizing opportunities in the changing marketplace. Unless you can change how you are differentiated, you will lose the potential rewards in the midst of this change. But, for instance, how could you have convinced engineers who were experts in analog mobile phone technology that they should learn digital technology? People must not only see that they must differentiate themselves in a new way; they must also see a clear path to becoming experts in the new technology.

Influencing Those Who Have Achieved Less in the Past

Those who have achieved less in the past often are cautious because their past experiences with change have not been good or because they are weary of change. They may have found areas of work in which they are moderately successful and, though they may not be totally pleased with their situation, they have settled for their places in life. They often resist change.

It's as if there's a law of human inertia that applies to both high and low achievers. Let's use a physics analogy.

Meaning and the physics of change. Galileo discovered a remarkable fact about motion: A body in motion will continue to move at the same speed in the same direction forever if it's not acted on by an inside or outside force. This is called Galileo's Law of Inertia, which would later become Isaac Newton's First Law of Motion.

If we could extend Newton's law to changes in humans and organizations, we might propose a second law of meaning.

The Second Law of Meaning: Many individuals and organizations will continue in the same direction, at the same speed, unless they are acted on by an inside or outside force. It's as if there's a law that says that the more meaning humans have invested in the way things are, the more they'll resist efforts to seize new opportunities that change the way things are.

Inertia and meaning. Some leaders assume that cautious people will be willing if they see the benefits of an opportunity. They're frustrated when others are skeptical and reluctant to change.

Because "the way things are" has high meaning for cautious people, they often resist change until they're in trouble. That's why the biggest need for progress and the largest opportunities are usually in organizations that cautious people are managing.

To get them to change, there must be dissatisfaction with the way things are; an urgent, compelling case for change; or a higher meaning.

You must help the cautious see that if they don't find and seize opportunities, others will pass them by and they will lose what they have. The best leaders also help them to find higher meaning in the new opportunity.

Help Cautious People Find Higher Meaning in a Mission

Steve Jobs has an extraordinary ability to get others to invest in a dream—to convert them into investors. He converted the Macintosh computer development team by promising that it would "put a dent in the universe."

So did Thomas Edison. One of his assistants said that Edison told them they were not inventing an electric light, they were dispelling night with its darkness from the arena of civilization.

At Gettysburg, after a battle that caused nearly 50,000 casualties, President Abraham Lincoln appealed to the highest meanings:

> FROM THESE HONORED DEAD WE TAKE INCREASED DEVOTION TO THAT CAUSE FOR WHICH THEY GAVE THE LAST FULL MEASURE OF DEVOTION—THAT WE HERE HIGHLY RESOLVE THAT THESE DEAD SHALL NOT HAVE DIED IN VAIN—THAT THIS NATION, UNDER GOD, SHALL HAVE A NEW BIRTH OF FREEDOM—AND THE GOVERNMENT OF THE PEOPLE, BY THE PEOPLE, FOR THE PEOPLE, SHALL NOT PERISH FROM THE EARTH.

These leaders converted cautious people by helping them to find the highest meanings in their missions and then helping them to find great opportunities to accomplish their missions.

The great, philosophical leader knows that shaping a stone has higher meaning when the stone is part of a cathedral. So he or she helps cautious masons see the cathedral they will be building.

In this vein, Louise Francesconi, the vice president of Raytheon's Missile Division, believes that the reward people get is seeing the vision and result as their own. She believes that people like to go to work when they feel that what they do is important and when they feel that they are the best in the world at what they do—when they feel they are the best missile makers in the world.

Leaders often fail when they keep people in the dark about the mission or when they expect them to do the job just because they're paid.

Actively Search for Higher Meaning with Cautious People

To find high meanings in which people will invest, the best leaders simply ask these kinds of questions:

- What do you feel is the most important issue facing you or your organization?
- What are the most important opportunities or threats for you in the future?
- What concerns you most right now?

Thus, the best leaders try to imagine how they would think and feel in other people's situations—essentially, they show empathy and compassion. They look for changes people will support. They ask, "If you could have any wish you wanted, what would you wish for?" and "What would you change if you could change anything you want?" During questioning, they regularly feed back to the person what they think he or she said, to make sure they have understood their meaning. Finally, they ask questions based on guesses they make about what people will willingly support.

Here are some recommendations for searching for meaning:

- Ask questions aimed at uncovering another's point of view, goals, thoughts, feelings, fears, joys, hopes, wishes, understandings, values, beliefs, and/or highest meanings.
- Acknowledge what you heard by restating what you believe the person said.
- Clarify and validate the person's point of view.
- Avoid analysis, judgment, coloration, amplification, diminishing, evaluation, or disagreement with the person's point of view.
- Carefully probe deeper when you find something that means a lot to the person.
- Acknowledge that you understand and respect what means a lot to him or her.
- Search for a benefit from the opportunity that will have high meaning for the person.
- If possible, redesign the opportunity so that it has high meaning for all who have a stake in it.

Finding out what means a lot to people is easier said than done. None of this is easy. But great leaders know it's worth it. They help cautious people find meaning in every step of the finding-and-seizing process. And they don't do certain things:

- They don't find opportunity for others; they help them to find it.
- They don't design or plan the opportunity for others; they help them to find opportunity that has high meaning for them.

- They don't implement for others; they support them and remove barriers as they implement.
- They don't provide the high meaning for others; they help them to find it.

> *Of a good leader, when his work is done, his aim fulfilled,*
> *they will all say, we did this ourselves.*
> —Lao-tzu, sixth century B.C.

Beyond Caution: Paths to New Expertise

Once you have helped cautious people see how they must change to seize new opportunities, you need to help them to see a path to developing the new expertise and, sometimes, help them find the passion they need to seize the new opportunities. In doing this, the best leaders set an example. Let's look at how one great businessman recently did this.

In the early 1980s, Andy Grove, the CEO of Intel, saw that his firm could no longer make profits in the computer memory business. He decided to move the company into becoming a producer of microprocessors. As soon as he made this decision, he spent a large portion of his time personally learning about microprocessors and how they make software work in computers. He asked both his internal people and outside software people to help him gain this new expertise. He told his executive staff that half of them had better become software experts within five years.

In other words, Grove set the example by changing his expertise and his passion. By 1985, microprocessor sales had grown, and Intel had closed eight memory plants and left the memory business. By 1996, it had more than 80 percent of the world's microprocessor business, more than $20 billion in sales, and twice its 1985 profit rate. Intel today is synonymous with microprocessors.

Finally, before they begin the seizing process, great leaders find common meaning and negotiate with those who might oppose any seizing of the opportunity.

Key 8

Negotiate in Advance with Potential Opposers

*Most people hate resistance. Because it is viewed so negatively,
people want to get over it. In the words of many articles on the subject,
people want to overcome resistance. This view is wrong.
Attempts to overcome it usually make it worse.*

—Rick Maurer, *Beyond the Wall of Resistance*

Great leaders know that opposers are simply protecting what has meaning to them or are champions of other opportunities that are competing for the same resources. So they study what the other opportunities offer and they search for ways to either convert the opposers or reduce their negative effects. However, like Galileo, leaders sometimes take the worst approach with those who oppose them. But this leads to a question: What's the best way to convert or reduce the negative effects of those who want to stop us from seizing opportunity? Let's look at the answer to this question.

What's the Best Way to Convert or Reduce the Negative Effects of Those Who Want to Stop Us From Seizing Opportunity?

The great innovators and achievers found three ways to convert or reduce the negative effects of those who wanted to stop them from seizing opportunities:

- Include opposing viewpoints.
- Find common meaning with opposers.
- Use force only as a last resort.

Include Opposing Viewpoints

In its short history, the United States has faced several crises that have threatened its existence. In each crisis, a leader emerged who was able to bring together opposing sides to seize the opportunity to survive. Let's look at two of these crises.

Hamilton faces the bankruptcy crisis. In April 1789, the newly formed U.S. government was sinking into bankruptcy. During the Revolutionary War, the federal government and the newly formed states had borrowed heavily to finance their efforts. Immediately after being sworn in as the first president, George Washington appointed Alexander Hamilton as secretary of the Treasury and asked him to tackle the problem.

Hamilton proposed that the federal government assume the debts of all the states. He believed this would forge the states together in a lasting union. But James Madison lashed out at Hamilton's proposal, saying that, because his home state and some other southern states had already paid off their wartime debts, they would be contributing to those states that hadn't done their duty. Many members of Congress saw that if Hamilton had his way, the federal government would become the central taxing authority. Congress voted down Hamilton's proposal.

But Hamilton didn't give up. He knew that the location for the nation's capital was a leverage point because it would bring great power, wealth, and population to the area chosen. At the time, there were two likely sites for the nation's capital: Philadelphia, because it had been the site of the Continental Congress and the drafting of the Declaration of Independence; and Virginia, the home state of Madison and Thomas Jefferson. He cut deals with the Pennsylvania and the Virginia delegations to vote for his proposal in exchange for his influence in locating the capital temporarily in Philadelphia, with a permanent location to be constructed later along the Potomac River.

With this tentative compromise in mind, Hamilton went to Jefferson and Madison and told them that the northern states were threatening secession if the capital was located in the South, but that he and President Washington would support the capital in Virginia if they and the southern states would support his proposal to have the federal government assume all wartime debts. They agreed, and the proposal passed in Congress. Jefferson said that he regretted this decision more than any other in his life, because he later realized that Hamilton's plan centralized great power in the federal government.

Hamilton was not only a great financial thinker; he was also a great negotiator. He knew that Madison and Jefferson would not risk having the northern states secede, no matter how badly they wanted the capital in Virginia. They needed his support to get the capital without secession, no matter how much they were opposed to his plan.

Kennedy faces the missile crisis. Another crisis took place in late 1962. U.S. spy planes flying over Cuba took pictures showing that the Cubans were building a nuclear missile installation from which they could reach most U.S. cities. President John F. Kennedy put a team together to analyze the situation and recommend action. By the end of the first day, it was nearly unanimous that the United States should launch a surprise air attack, followed by an invasion.

But Kennedy knew that Soviet soldiers at the missile installation would be killed by air strikes, which would escalate the situation to a U.S.–Soviet conflict. He and his brother Robert ("Bobby") remembered a disastrous decision they had made 18 months earlier, when they decided to secretly help a band of Cuban exiles invade Cuba at the Bay of Pigs. The Central Intelligence Agency (CIA) had predicted that people in Cuba would join the invading force and then rise up and overthrow Cuban President Fidel Castro.

But the Bay of Pigs invasion had been a disaster. The Cuban military captured the invaders and then humiliated them by parading them through the streets of Havana. When President Kennedy appointed a blue ribbon committee to find out what had gone wrong, the committee members said that the president was to blame because he decided on an answer before weighing alternatives. They also said that his brother Bobby had shut off all Cabinet opposition to the invasion. The brothers were so shaken by this report that they changed their fundamental approach to decision making—never again deciding on an answer until all the options had been developed and all opposers' viewpoints had been considered.

So, during the missile crisis, Bobby Kennedy asked the team to come up with other responses. On the third day of struggling for options, someone suggested a limited blockade as a first step. Some members of the group thought that a limited blockade would open a window for negotiation. Others saw it as a first step toward an air strike, an ultimatum. Eventually, the whole group agreed on a limited blockade as a first step.

The next day, President Kennedy presented the plan to the Joint Chiefs of Staff, saying that the blockade would serve as an ultimatum, followed by air strikes if needed. He talked to the congressional leaders and then went on worldwide television and radio to announce a shipping quarantine of Cuba. He said that ships entering the quarantine zone would be stopped and searched. He warned that if any missiles were fired from Cuba, the United States would launch a nuclear strike against the Soviet Union.

In the next few days, the world held its breath as Soviet ships headed toward the blockade. At the last minute, Soviet Premier Nikita Khrushchev turned the ships around and offered to remove the missiles in return for a U.S. promise not to invade Cuba. When one of Kennedy's team heard that the ships had turned around, he said, "We've just had a showdown, and the other guy blinked."

Recently declassified Soviet and U.S. documents indicate that the situation was more dangerous than the Kennedys imagined. Secret memos from Khrushchev show he was worried that he couldn't control Soviet officers in Cuba. The CIA estimated Soviet troop strength in Cuba at only a few thousand lightly armed men. But Soviet documents reveal that there were 40,000 Soviet troops in Cuba at the time, equipped with battlefield nuclear weapons. An air strike or invasion could have triggered Armageddon.

President Kennedy learned the importance of listening to opposing views and negotiating for solutions that took advantage of the collective wisdom of his advisers.

Find Common Meaning With Potential Opposers

Unwilling investors have a tendency to oppose new opportunities, as is shown in figure 8-1, where they are represented by the lower circle drawn with the dotted line. The use of good techniques can move them from this opposition up to a more neutral position, shown by the shaded circle. Avoiding this group or the use of poor techniques can cause strong opposition to the opportunity that you are pursuing.

In facing crises, both Hamilton and Kennedy used powerful negotiation techniques to bring opposing sides together—in effect, creating a win-win situation (see the sidebar). Earlier in the book, we presented some recommendations for searching for meaning. The same recommendations apply to negotiating with opposers, with the addition of the following:

- Assume that opposers have legitimate reasons for their positions and their interests.
- Find the minimum terms that each opposer will accept.
- Find a common need or want.
- Negotiate a win-win plan if you can.
- Think of alternatives if you can't get a settlement. What will you do if either side refuses to budge, walks away, or escalates its opposition? Is time on your side or against you?

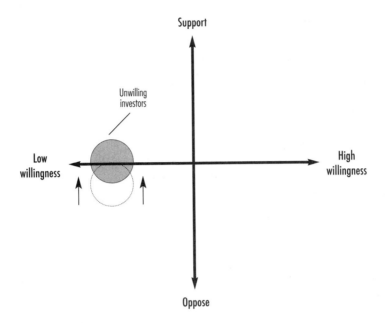

Figure 8-1. Unwilling investors and willingness to invest.

There are those who feel that win-win thinking is weak-minded—that winning is the only thing. They believe that the best negotiators are those who can negotiate the lion's share. They view negotiation as a contest where the "best" party wins at others' expense. The tactics of such win-lose negotiators are to negotiate from a position of strength, to set their demands so high initially that the final negotiated settlement is biased in their favor, and to act as if time is on their side.

For nearly 100 years, beginning with violent strikes against the auto companies and recent strikes in American sports, union-management contract negotiations have been plagued by adversarial negotiating. On the one hand, these are usually costly

---

Steven Covey says that win-win leaders see life more as a cooperative —not a competitive—arena, and that win-win thinking "is based on a belief that there is plenty for everybody, that one person's success is not achieved at the expense or exclusion of the success of others." See his book *The 7 Habits of Highly Successful People* (New York: Fireside, 1989).

to all stakeholders. Many have led to permanent losses of jobs, the termination of unions, company bankruptcies, and the loss of customers. In other words, there is a high risk that adversarial negotiation will end in lose-lose. On the other hand, some believe that *every* opportunity creates winners and losers. The expression, "You can't make an omelet without cracking a few eggs" is often used to justify this position.

Win-win negotiators view negotiation as another form of co-creation.

The toughest leaders don't negotiate with the opposition; they fire them. That sends a message. Then everyone's willing to do whatever it takes to keep his or her job. However, fear won't convert someone into a willing investor, especially if he or she has other opportunities. Fearful people may do what it takes to survive; but instead of devoting their creativity to seizing the opportunity, they may devote it to quietly sabotaging it. Even worse, creative people will leave organizations that dictate what they must do. The best leaders design the opportunity with all involved so that everyone gains from seizing it. That's win-win thinking.

Over a period of time, an organization that uses the keys to mobilize people's support increases its number of eager investors and their overall willingness to change. At the same time, it decreases the number of people in the organization who are opposed to change. Over time, as the organization increases its number of eager investors, it sees the opportunities in the changing world and creates its own future. But an organization that fears and opposes change will have its future created for it.

In extreme cases, opposers will put you in prison or kill you if you seize the opportunity they oppose. In such cases, it takes great heroism to begin the seizing process. Occasionally a hero will arise, risk all, and plant seeds for change that profoundly alter the course of history.

A hero arises. One great hero arose in China in 1978, when farmers in the village of Xiaogang were starving. Chinese law forced them to turn their crops over to the government in exchange for such small amounts of grain that they could not feed their families.

Witnessing this starvation, Yan Hongchang, the village leader, decided that death by starvation was so terrible that any punishment the government would inflict for violating the law could not be worse. He persuaded 18 farmers to sign a pact that divided their land into family plots. They promised to turn their production quotas in to be given to the government, but they would keep whatever remained—a violation of Chinese law. The agreement also said: "In the case of failure, we are prepared for death or prison, and other commune members vow to raise our children until they are 18 years old."

In 1979, the leader of the commune of 10,000 members, which included Yan's village, accused the village of "digging up the cornerstone of the Revolution." In desperation, Yan went to Chen, his county's Communist Party secretary and a man with a reputation for having an open mind, and begged for help. Chen had heard that the group's harvests were good, so he agreed to protect the village as long as the practice didn't spread. Eventually, however, word of the violation made its way to Beijing and to China's new premier, Deng Xiaoping. The villagers braced for the worst.

Deng surprised everyone. Instead of meting out punishment, he was so impressed with what the villagers had accomplished that he applauded them and directed that they be used as an example of what the Chinese farmer could do.

From heroism to pragmatism. Years later, when Deng reflected on the rise of the village entrepreneurs, he was especially candid. He said, "It was if a strange army appeared in the countryside, making and selling a huge variety of products. This is not the achievement of our central government. . . . This was not something I figured out. . . . This was a surprise."

The new philosophy of pragmatism that Deng sanctioned—believing that a method is good if it produces good economic results—has spread throughout China and is fueling the largest industrial revolution in history.

So if the opposers can destroy your life, it helps to seize an opportunity that is also a "win" for them. It also helps to have a temporary protector to shield you until the rewards are delivered.

Use Force Only as a Last Resort

When leaders become frustrated with opposition, they may react with force. The problem is the word "force"! Rick Maurer, a change consultant, says that people lose their effectiveness when they react to resistance by

- using power
- manipulating those who oppose
- applying the force of reason
- ignoring resistance
- playing off relationships
- making deals
- killing the messenger.

There is a common thread in these reactions: They're all intended to overcome resistance. But these reactions don't sell the opportunity to cautious investors, nor will they help you find common meaning and negotiate with opposers. On this topic, you might want to read more by Maurer, who introduced us to the concept of embracing resistance. He has concluded from his research that the ability to embrace resistance is a key secret of those who are able to go beyond the "wall of resistance." See his book *Beyond the Wall of Resistance* (Austin: Bard Books, 1996). This leads to a third law of meaning, which applies to opposers.

The Third Law of Meaning: The more we force opposers to give up what has high meaning to them, the more they may resist. Leaders are at their best when they're co-creating, selling, and finding common meaning. They search for meanings that the opportunity can have for all with a stake in it. They encourage people to express their needs, hopes, aspirations, concerns, and fears. They relax in the face of opposing views, letting others know that it is OK to express opposition.

Do you, the reader, have negative feelings when

- your views are questioned or attacked?
- your motives or intentions are denounced?
- others don't trust you?
- they say they can't or won't do what's asked of them?
- they say it can't be done?
- they try to sabotage the effort you are leading?

Summary of Keys 5 through 8

To summarize keys 5 through 8, great leaders

- search for the highest meanings of those who have a stake in the opportunity
- co-create the opportunity with them so that it produces the largest rewards they can get for their investment
- sell opportunity to cautious people by helping them see how they must change to seize new opportunities
- negotiate with opposers to minimize their resistance.

Figure 8-2 shows typical results from effectively mobilizing support to reduce the negative effects of unwilling investors, the large effects of selling to cautious investors, and creating enthusiastic support from highly willing eager investors.

Great leaders help all stakeholders find and seize the highest-leverage opportunities with the highest meaning.

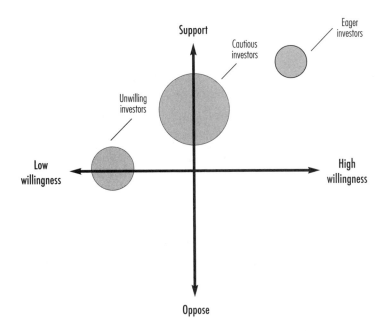

Figure 8-2. Eager, cautious, and unwilling investors and willingness to invest.

Building a Bridge

Between finding an opportunity and seizing an opportunity, there is a great canyon that swallows most opportunity finders. Building a bridge across this canyon is the work of leaders, designers, and implementers. The seizing process is like a military battle. You can plan it and manage it, but once the battle begins, you must lead it in a high-leverage, high-meaning way, as discussed in detail in part III of this book.

Self-Evaluation Exercise

Below, list the key people—the stakeholders—who were involved in your last project or endeavor in the left-hand column. Then check the box that indicates the type of stakeholder they are—eager, cautious, or opposer. Finally, check the boxes of any approaches you used with them on the seven right-hand columns.

	Stakeholders	Type of Stakeholder			Approach used						
		Eager	Cautious	Opposer	1 Consulted them early	2 Collaborated with them extensively in early formative phases	3 Drew out and answered objections and concerns	4 Used sales and influencing techniques	5 Found their higher meanings and related project to those meanings	6 Searched for common needs or settled for terms they would accept	7 Negotiated for win-win or some equitable solution
Example	Sue Thomas	✓						✓	✓		

The approach used for eager stakeholders should be mostly from columns 1 and 2. Likewise, for cautious stakeholders, columns 3, 4, and 5 should be used. For opposers, the approach should be from columns 6 and 7.

Part III

Seize Great Opportunities

To rank as a masterpiece, a work of art must stand as a supreme and timeless accomplishment. Creating one work this extraordinary could be the crowning glory of any artist's life. And among the few who have achieved the remarkable distinction of producing a masterpiece in more than one branch of the arts, Michelangelo Buonarotti stands almost totally alone. His vast number of creations includes the vivid biblical scenes that grace the ceiling of the Sistine Chapel and the heroic marble statue of David. During his own lifetime, he was called divine.

—Biography: Michelangelo, Artist and Man, A&E Television

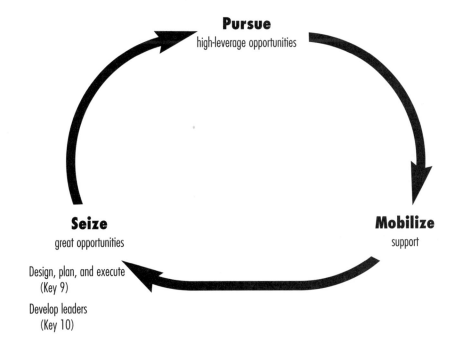

Pursue
high-leverage opportunities

Mobilize
support

Seize
great opportunities

Design, plan, and execute
(Key 9)

Develop leaders
(Key 10)

Between finding and seizing an opportunity is a great canyon that swallows most opportunity finders. In researching this book, we analyzed how more than 100 highly successful people bridged that canyon. We've categorized what they did into the two most powerful keys to great execution, shown in the diagram on the previous page.

Great execution begins with design, and the next leader is a master of it.

Key 9

Design, Plan, and Execute

Think of the end before the beginning.

—Leonardo da Vinci

In 1954, Sol Price, a young lawyer, opened a discount store. Everything went well until he discounted bottled alcoholic beverages. He was threatened with jail and hit with a major lawsuit from the alcoholic beverage industry. He fought back and survived a hurricane of lawsuits. He narrowly escaped jail, but he won against all odds and built a $300 million chain of stores called FedMart. In 1974, he sold the chain with the agreement that he and his sons would continue as top executives. Within a year, the new owner fired them.

Price felt betrayed. Nevertheless, as the great achievers always did, he searched until he found another opportunity. He found that small retailers couldn't make any profit selling cigarettes, candy, and soft drinks. Wholesalers were charging them a 25 percent markup because their orders were small. Price and his son Robert believed that if they could design a wholesale business that was profitable at a 10 percent markup on small orders, they could capture the small retailer market. For more on the Prices' story, see *Profiles of Genius* by Gene N. Landrum (Buffalo: Prometheus Books, 1993).

Why Design Matters—and Is Natural

After finding the opportunity, Sol and Robert Price used a design process that is used by great designers and anyone who wants to seize opportunities. We know that a lot of people don't feel capable of design. But we are natural designers. Watch a child build with blocks or plan a tea party. That's design. Whether you plant a garden or create a plan to attract investors, you're designing. We design our lives, or they're designed for us. But many opportunity finders fail to seize opportunity because they don't have a good design process.

Once the opportunity has been found, the designer's job is to create whatever is needed—a new product, process, system, or organization—that will fulfill the opportunity. To do this, the designer must answer three questions:

- What is the purpose of the design, and who benefits?
- How do we create the best design?
- How do we ensure that the design will work?

In our research, we studied the processes of the best designers and boiled them down to three phases, each answering one of these questions. A great designer will consider the first question to be the most important one.

First Phase: What Is the Purpose of the Design, and Who Benefits?

The great designer Leonardo da Vinci once said, "Always think of the end before the beginning." Although it may seem obvious that the first phase should focus on the end purpose, often the questions about purpose and beneficiaries are not well-answered before design work begins. Steven Covey identifies "beginning with the end in mind" as a habit of highly successful people and a guideline for life design; see his book *The 7 Habits of Highly Successful People* (New York: Fireside, 1989).

The Prices' end purpose was a business that made a profit providing small orders of name-brand goods, at a 10 percent markup, to small retailers, so they could compete with large retailers. To meet that purpose, their design would have to eliminate credit card fees, costs of giving people credit, shipping-breakdown costs, trucking costs, delivery costs, and outside-sales costs. Also, inventory and leasing costs would have to be low.

The first phase of design always involves finding the purpose. For example, see the sidebar on Sidney Lumet's filmmaking.

Before they finish the first phase, master designers analyze their work to check that the design concept matches their purpose. Here's a checklist used by the great achievers:

- Is the opportunity high leverage?
- Is there a real or perceived need for what we're designing? Does the design have high meaning and high value to customers?

- Do we have a good estimate of the benefits to the customer?
- Have we designed the product with enough uniqueness to attract customers?
- Do we know the target customers or target market?
- Have we estimated correctly the size of the target market?
- Have we covered the right-size market with the design? Have we tried to cover too broad a market? Have we designed features into the product or service that have no value to the target customers?
- Have we tested the basic concept or a model of the design with potential customers?

As we'll see, Sol Price initially failed on one checkpoint. He overestimated the size of the market for his business. Once the designer knows the purpose of the design and its beneficiaries, he or she goes on to answer the second question.

Second Phase: How Do We Create the Best Design?

In this phase, the designer must decide what functions the design must perform to meet its purpose and what ideas, patterns, forms, and processes can be combined to provide the new functions and be practical for implementation.

Sol and Robert Price designed not only what functions their business would perform but also what it would not do. By selling only name brands that were advertised nationally, they could keep advertising costs low. They could trim the costs of receiving, stocking, and inventory by carrying only 3,000 brand-name products. A typical Kmart at that time carried 100,000 brand-name products. Sol said that he set the limit because "you can't be everything to everybody." This wisdom applies

---

The award-winning movie maker Sidney Lumet has directed more than 30 feature films, including *Twelve Angry Men, Serpico, Murder on the Orient Express, The Verdict, The Pawnbroker,* and *Dog Day Afternoon.* Lumet says his first phase begins with asking the screenwriter: "What is this story about? What did you see? What was your intention? Ideally, if we do this well, what do you hope the audience will feel, think, sense? In what mood do you want them to leave the theater?'" He says the answers to these questions determine how the movie will be cast; how it will look; how it will be made, edited, musically scored, mixed, and titled. For more, see Lumet's book *Making Movies* (New York: Vintage Books, 1996).

to designs of all products and services that have high costs of marketing, production, and distribution. (It does not apply to the Internet economy, where the costs of marketing, producing, and distribution may be so low that it may be economical to carry a million products or services, as do eBay and Amazon.)

The Prices also designed what functions the customer would perform. By having customers pay with cash or a check, they could eliminate credit card fees and accounts-receivable costs. By having customers buy goods in bulk packs, they could eliminate shipping-breakdown costs. By having customers pick up their own merchandise at their warehouse, they could eliminate delivery costs. By placing the warehouse in a low-rent area, they could keep overhead costs low.

In the second phase, most designers use new technology only when the new technology is proven and is needed to create the best design. Sol Price didn't need new technologies, such as computer programs and automated warehouses, to make his initial design meet his purpose. Great designers first try forms or processes that fit existing technologies.

Developing new technology often takes large resources and long times. Saturn succeeded in designing a new car, a new factory, and new manufacturing processes; shaping a new workforce and management philosophy; developing new suppliers; creating a new distribution system; and fundamentally improving the way in which cars are sold. But it took seven years and it cost Saturn billions before it became profitable. Only a company like General Motors could have financed it.

When Honda moved to the United States, it duplicated a car, a process, and a factory it already had in Japan. It carefully selected a workforce and suppliers that it felt would readily adopt Japanese manufacturing methods. It sent workers to Japan to learn the process. It was up and running profitably in less than two years.

Many designers fail when they try to do too much in the second phase.

Optimize the Whole: Zoom In, Zoom Out

During the second phase, great designers optimize the whole. Frederick P. Brooks Jr., the chief designer of IBM's 360, the most successful mainframe computer of all time, says that unity of design is the most important design consideration; see his book *The Mythical Man Month* (Reading, MA: Addison Wesley, 1975). To achieve unity of design, "the overall design must meet the intent or purpose of the opportunity" and "each part should be aligned and designed in best relationship to each other and to the purpose of the overall design."

Master designers do not optimize the whole by optimizing the parts. They first optimize the whole and then they optimize the parts to fit the optimum whole. To do this, they begin at the highest level, then move rapidly from upper levels of the design to lower levels and back to upper levels. This ensures that the forms and functions of the smaller components of the design fit the overall design, and vice versa. For example, Edison

- could think one moment of providing power from a massive electrical distribution system
- could think the next moment of the design of the generator that would be needed to create the power
- and, a moment later, could think of a design detail in the rotor of the generator.

Master designers move up and down across the various levels of a design as often as 50 times an hour. This is called "zoom in, zoom out." For more on this, see the article "A Field Study of the Software Design Process for Large Systems" by Bill Curtis, Herb Krasner, and Neil Iscoe, *Communications of ACM* (issued by the Association for Computing Machinery), November 1988.

Sol Price and Michelangelo could see the forest one moment, a small leaf on a single tree the next moment, and switch back to the forest in the next moment.

The third phase answers the question: "How do we ensure that the design will work?" It consists of experimental test, analysis, and redesign.

Third Phase: How Do We Ensure That the Design Will Work?

Sol and Robert rented an abandoned airplane hangar, put shelves in it, put a checkout counter at one end, and named it Price Club. They purchased name brand items in bulk. They had suppliers deliver them and put them on the shelves. They had shoppers load their own items off the shelves, bring them to the counter, pay cash, and carry them out. Robert Price came up with the idea of selling annual memberships for $25, causing the Wall Street analyst Michael Exstein to remark, "It was unimaginable, this idea that you could charge people to shop."

As with many designers who venture into the unknown, their first test proved that their design didn't work. In its first year, Price Club could not attract enough customers to be profitable, and it lost so much money that Sol was threatened with bankruptcy.

With time and money running out, Sol analyzed what was wrong with the design. He concluded that the design of the store, the product selection, and the cost structure were right. He admitted that his decision to sell only to retailers was killing the business. At bankruptcy's door, the Prices changed the design. They opened the store to government employees and self-employed individuals. The chance to buy wholesale goods through their business and use them personally was irresistible to self-employed people, and Price Club was stampeded with applications. By 1981, sales had reached $230 million.

Within 10 years, the Prices had 25 stores generating $2.6 billion a year. Their design was so successful that Sam Walton copied it and called it Sam's Club. Walton said, "I've stolen or borrowed as many ideas from Sol Price as from anybody else"; see the book *Made in America* by Sam Walton and John Huey (New York: Doubleday, 1992). Pace, Macro, and Costco also copied the design, and Price Club merged with Costco in 1994.

The second and third phases of the design process often are repeated until the design meets the purpose and is easier to implement. Occasionally, it may be necessary to return to the first phase and modify the original purpose, as Sol Price did.

General Principles of Experimental Testing

A general principle of experimental design and testing that great designers use is to identify the high-risk parts of the design and redesign to eliminate the risk early in the design process. Then test the new designs under the worst conditions and make corrections. The earlier in the design process that you test a design, the better—as shown in the sidebar on the IDEO Corporation.

Most great design organizations build models of the product as early as possible to test them. With that, and some of the other early-learning processes, they shortened their time to develop new products by 50 percent. That helps them keep their position as the new product leader in their market.

Master designers spend a great deal of time imagining what can go wrong with the design. Then they focus on the worst possible failures and design test processes and equipment that will stress the design in a way that induces the failures. They put early models of the design through the tests, and they find and fix the defects. They conduct reviews with potential investors—especially customers—to get feedback. The best designers eliminate almost all problems they discover in the test process before they finalize a design.

The IDEO Corporation leads the world in industrial design. Its designs range from high-tech blood analyzers to stand-up toothpaste tubes. Once it understands the market, the technology, and the constraints on the problem, IDEO observes people in real situations in that market, to find out what makes them tick—what confuses them, what they like, what they hate, and where they have latent needs not addressed by current products and services. IDEO's designers visualize people using the product and then build a series of quick prototypes to evaluate the design in the hands of customers. The general manager, Tom Kelley, says the designers try not to get attached to the first few prototypes because they know they'll change. For more on IDEO, see Kelley's book *The Art of Innovation* (New York: Doubleday, 2001).

Because of the importance of "early test and build," many organizations have completely redesigned the first processes in their product development cycles. For instance, the Powertrain Division of General Motors has developed very sophisticated computer-design programs that allow it to design engine components on the computer and then test them on the computer under simulated conditions. It also has developed new processes that allow it to build a first prototype of an engine part in hours, rather than weeks or months. Powertrain then measures and tests these rapidly made prototypes to correct any design defects before finalizing the design. As a result, the quality of GM's engines has greatly improved over the past 10 years.

Find Opportunity First

It's worth reemphasizing a point made earlier. The best designers first search for a great opportunity for success because identifying problems and solving them is low-leverage activity unless you know that those problems are the largest obstacles to your success; see Peter F. Drucker's book *Managing for Results* (New York: Harper, 1964). Then the best designers focus only on problems that stand in the way of success.

Thinking Skills

Great designers use thinking skills—such as imagining, synthesizing, testing, and analyzing—in all phases of their design and problem-solving processes. Synthesis, or putting parts together to form a functional whole, is usually the most difficult thinking skill to learn. It's one matter to analyze what makes an automobile work; it is far more difficult to synthesize hundreds of parts into a well-performing machine. Can the reader see where Sol and Robert Price used these thinking processes to find and seize a wholesale business opportunity? For more on thinking, see the sidebar.

When the design work is completed, implementation begins. To achieve the full potential of the design, we should focus resources—such as people, money, and expertise—at high-leverage points. A high-leverage point is where we can spend a small amount of resources to produce large benefits. This is fully discussed in the next section.

Each of us can recall a moment in our life when a different decision or a different choice would have led to an entirely different future. So it was with Bill Gates in the summer of 1980.

Rapidly Seizing Opportunities at High-Leverage Points

In 1980, IBM decided to build a personal computer. It also decided that, to get it to the market fast with a competitive cost, it would have to be built with components and software obtained from outside IBM. Jack Sams was given the job of finding software suppliers. Sams knew that Microsoft, a small company with 32 employees, supplied most of the software for personal computers on the market. So he called Bill Gates, the president of Microsoft, and asked for a meeting. Gates said, "How about two weeks?" Sams said, "How about tomorrow?"

The next day, Sams flew to Bellevue, Washington. As he exited an elevator at Microsoft, he was met by what appeared to be an awkward, teenage office boy in a poorly fitting suit. The boy kept pushing his dirty, wire-rimmed glasses up on his

---

If someone wants to increase their thinking skills, we recommend the book *The Teaching of Thinking*, by Raymond S. Nickerson, David N. Perkins, and Edward E. Smith (Hillsdale, NY: Lawrence Erlbaum, 1985). But, as we note in the main text, the highest-leverage way to learn anything is in pursuing a future opportunity. So work with a great opportunity finder if you can. Engage in a project requiring design and problem solving, and work with a good problem solver on the project.

---

nose. Sams soon discovered that this was Gates. Gates rocked back and forth during the meeting, appearing to be scatterbrained. Microsoft's offices were tiny by IBM standards; they didn't make a good first impression. IBM asked Gates to sign a nondisclosure agreement; Gates signed it without hesitation.

In a three-hour meeting, Gates impressed Sams with his grasp of PC hardware, software, and the industry. Sams said that Gates was one of the smartest people he had ever met. Sams told Gates he wanted him to provide the disk operating system (DOS) for the new computer. Gates surprised Sams by saying he didn't supply operating systems and referring him to DRI, which had a popular operating system at that time.

When IBM's people visited DRI, the president was unavailable, and his business manager refused to sign the nondisclosure agreement, so under IBM's rules of engagement, there could be no discussion. After hours of stalemate, the IBM representatives left.

Sams called Gates again and told him that Microsoft had to supply an operating system or IBM wouldn't buy Microsoft's language programs. Gates felt that operating systems were not his expertise and that developing an operating system would pull resources away from where Microsoft made its money. Besides, if Microsoft entered the operating-system business, DRI might react by entering the language business.

However, pressed with an ultimatum, Gates decided to do it. He knew another developer who had an operating system. A visit with the other developer confirmed that he would sell his operating system. Gates immediately called Sams to tell him he had it. They discussed whether Microsoft or IBM should buy it. It's not clear whether either of them knew the significance of the ownership of that piece of software. It was decided that Microsoft would buy it, and that decision ultimately drove Microsoft's stock value to $400 billion. For Gates and Sams, this was a defining moment, a high-leverage point in time.

Sams believed that, if IBM bought the software, the company would bungle it. He wanted Microsoft to be responsible for integrating all the software. Gates wanted to be known as the company that supplied IBM's personal computer software. He knew that was a high-leverage opportunity and that the purchase of the operating system was a high-leverage point, so he bought the software for $50,000—a lot of money at that time.

Referring to this leverage point, the writer-analyst Paul Carrol said, "Sams may be right that IBM would have bungled DOS, but IBM, in not being able to seize that chance, put themselves at a horrible disadvantage." In defense of Sams, leverage points are fleeting; you have to act quickly, and if he had brought DOS inside IBM, that probably would have delayed IBM's introduction of the PC by at least a year.

There would be other high-leverage points on Microsoft's journey and, nearly every time, Gates took the right action at the right moment. Later, Gates sold nonexclusive rights to IBM to use the MS-DOS software. IBM was confident that the software was useless without a special chip it had designed into the computer. Later, Compaq Computer reverse-engineered the IBM chip and produced an IBM clone. As others developed clones, Microsoft sold them the MS-DOS software, which eventually became the basis for Windows, now the standard software on most of the world's personal computers.

Later, IBM spent hundreds of millions of dollars suing Compaq and Microsoft, trying to reclaim the MS-DOS software that Microsoft had bought. IBM lost nearly every suit. At the time of the leverage point, Microsoft had 32 employees and a few million dollars in sales, and IBM had 340,000 employees and $26 billion in sales. But Microsoft had the inside expertise and was led by Gates, a master of high-leverage opportunity and high-leverage points.

This is also an example of a power insider hiring an expert insider. The irony is that IBM got the expertise but Gates got the power. Another example of seizing at high leverage points took place at one of the premier golf equipment manufacturers.

Long before PING Inc., was known for its excellence in designing and manufacturing golf equipment, its founder, Karsten Solheim, was working for General Electric in 1953 and playing golf with a borrowed set of clubs. He was frustrated with the difficulty of putting straight. But he used his mechanical engineering background along with an observation on the construction of tennis rackets. He reasoned that if tennis rackets were weighted around the perimeter of the head of the racket, the same concept could be used to design a putter. As soon as he knew that he had an invention that improved putting accuracy, he acquired a loan for machining equipment and set up operations in his garage.

Karsten Solheim grew his enterprise to 2,000 employees, with Forbes estimating his net worth at $400 million; see *Karsten's Way* by Tracy Sumner (Chicago: Northfield Publishing, 2000). Nevertheless, in the mid-1990s, modern market pressures increased the demand for more variety, newer technology, higher performance, and continually evolving design appeal, placing the entire corporation in an uncomfortable position. PING was faced with high overhead and slipping sales. The task ahead was formidable for the executive team members. They found themselves in a position where maintaining the legacy of years past would no longer suffice. They would need to face the daunting task of reinventing something that had worked flawlessly for decades.

John A. Solheim, one of Karsten's three sons, was promoted to CEO of PING in 1995, and he began the process of creating a leaner, more efficient corporation. He focused PING's business by eliminating activities that were not directly supporting the manufacture of golf equipment or didn't support corporate values. He also restructured the existing departments and leveraged the fitting system that PING is famous for. In 2001, he had only one major department that was still in need of transformation, the engineering department. He appointed his son, John K. Solheim, as vice president of engineering to tackle this task (figure 9-1).

The PING engineering department was in need of improvements relating to the speed of time to market and rate of innovation and productivity. Taking a design concept to production in two years was the state of the art in the 1980s; but in 2001, the design could be obsolete before the first piece came off the production line. Also, launching a single line of products every other year would no longer compete with the faster moving competitors. PING needed to launch products four times faster than before. It would also need to attempt the unnerving task of updating a look of a product that has been branded with a distinctive and differentiated look. The speed of innovation and the product complexity would also need to increase substantially if PING was to regain its market dominance in premium fitted clubs.

Figure 9-1. John A. Solheim, John K. Solheim, and Karsten Solheim (left to right). (Photograph courtesy of PING, Inc.)

John K. Solheim quickly began to get the right people using the right tools with the most efficient processes and procedures. He hired talented people to lead teams and reorganized the existing PING engineering department structure. He also purchased productivity tools such as Pro/Engineer to improve computer-aided design productivity and launched lean initiatives to improve processes. He then arranged the design teams into a flat structure that had leadership but deemphasized hierarchy and allowed all the company's designers to sell their ideas to management with an unprecedented ability to manage their idea from design through production.

The final improvements decreased their design concept to production time from 24 to 9 months and increased the number of products introduced each year from 3 to 14 while maintaining the same staffing levels. During this same period, PING launched the number one driver, the number one iron, and the number two putter brands. When asked about the changes that PING has been through, John K. Solheim explains: "Looking back at all the improvements we've made, I credit our success to having the right people, providing them with the right tools, and creating efficient processes." Leaders always put the right people in the right high-leverage places so that they can seize opportunity quickly.

To learn how to find and seize opportunities using high-leverage points, the leader must answer these questions:

- What is a high-leverage point?
- How do we find high-leverage points?
- How do we act at multiple points in an organized campaign?

What Is a High-Leverage Point?

A high-leverage point in a system is where a small action produces a large change in operation and output. There are many varieties of high-leverage points, from the up button in an elevator to a bottleneck in a manufacturing process. Learning to find high-leverage points is both a science and an art.

An Indianapolis 500 race car has small wings on each side at the front. The Indy winner Bobby Rahal says that changing the angle on the left-front aerodynamic wing by one-tenth of one degree might get you around the Speedway one-tenth of a second faster. At the end of 200 laps at Indianapolis, that's a difference of 20 seconds, which is enough to win or lose the race. Rahal says that if you can figure out enough of these minute adjustments so that you can gain a few seconds per lap, you can run away with the Indy 500. The angle of each wing is a high-leverage point because a very small change in the angle makes a large difference in the outcome of the race.

How Do We Find High-Leverage Points?

To repeat, a high-leverage point is where spending a small amount of resources produces large benefits. Peter Senge, who has researched the dynamics of systems, says that "the areas of highest leverage are often the least obvious." For example, a very large force is needed to change the direction of a moving ship, if you are pushing its front in the direction in which you want it to go. But a small force to change the angle of the rudder will turn the ship. The rudder is an example of an obvious leverage point. However, the tiny trim tab on a boat is a not-so-obvious leverage point. An even smaller change in the position of the trim tab increases or decreases how much effort it will take to move the rudder.

Because of the great value of high-leverage points, it's very important to learn how to find them. Let's look at several examples.

Edison, Master of Leverage Points

In the movie *Edison the Man*, Spencer Tracy, playing Edison, is sitting at his desk early one morning, after struggling through the night trying to find a suitable filament. He is holding a piece of sewing thread in his hand. "We're going to use carbon," he says to the men just coming to work. After he gives instructions to one of the men about how to impregnate the thread with carbon and bake it, the man says, "It's too delicate, Tom, I'm afraid we'll break it." "Try it anyway," Edison says. Another man says, "But we've tried carbon before." "Not carbonized thread," Edison says. "That isn't very scientific," the man says. "I told you we had to leave science behind. Now come on," Tom says, motioning for them to get on with it.

They prepare the thread as Edison has instructed and, lo and behold, though all previous filaments had burned out in minutes, the lamp burns continually through that night and the following night. In that dramatic moment, Edison gives the world the gift of electric lighting.

This story reinforces the myth that breakthroughs come magically. As we've said above, we've been led to believe that if we simply free the imaginative and playful children's minds within us, we will be able to create visions.

But on the contrary, before Edison devised the first filaments for his lamp, his physicist, Francis Upton, already had determined that the filament must have an electrical resistance of about 100 ohms, have a melting point over 6,000 degrees Fahrenheit, and be extremely thin and long without being too fragile. The eventual focus on carbon was no accident, in that Edison knew its properties and had worked with it in developing an improved telephone voice-piece. But even after his team narrowed the search to extremely thin carbon filaments, the search lasted for the best part of 1879.

Edison and his team mentally "saw" their solutions long before they ever realized them in the laboratory. This narrowed the scope from millions of experiments to thousands. In other words, they knew millions of things that wouldn't work, so they didn't need to try them. Long before the "magical" experiment took place, they knew which materials and experiments would have the highest leverage.

The highest-leverage opportunity for Edison was creating a commercial electrical lighting system. To accomplish this, he knew that he would have to develop all the parts of the generators, lamps, and distribution system. Of these developments, he knew that finding a suitable lamp was the high-leverage development and that the major problem would be inventing a high-resistance, high-temperature, yet durable filament. Finally, he knew that the highest-leverage action was to design, build, and mount the filaments and create vacuums around them (figure 9-2).

Realizing the importance of the highest-leverage action, Edison invented a self-contained, fast-turnaround laboratory to do it. He staffed it with

- chemists who could carbonize his filaments
- physicists who could calculate from the properties of materials whether they had a chance of working
- an expert on high vacuum
- a glass blower
- an expert on glass-to-metal seals.

This team could start with an idea for a filament in the morning, build it that afternoon, and test it that evening. The scientists were able to test thousands of materials, filament cross-sections, carbonizing techniques, dozens of vacuum methods and glass-to-metal seals, and hundreds of wire supports for the filaments.

Two years after he started his lighting project, Edison ran out of money just as they found the answer. If he hadn't searched for the highest leverage in the beginning, he never would have made it. Rather than 2 years, it would have taken 10 years to develop a suitable filament.

The search for high-leverage points begins once you have a vision of a great opportunity. Starting at the highest level of the opportunity, you systematically work your way down, level by level, selecting the highest-leverage points at each level. Then, to make sure you have identified a genuine high-leverage point, you need to ask

Figure 9-2. Thomas Alva Edison (© Corbis)

whether a small change at that point will make a large difference in your ability to seize the high-level opportunity. Edison knew that if his team could invent a suitable filament, he could create a commercially successful electric lighting system. You need to understand the leverage point well enough to perform the right action on it.

Churchill also was a master of leverage-point decisions, especially in crisis. Two of his most important decisions at leverage points took place shortly after he became the prime minister of the United Kingdom.

Crisis Leverage Points and Winston Churchill

The first decision came just as Hitler's armored divisions invaded France. The French begged Churchill for British fighter planes to help in their defense. Churchill believed that the French would lose, even with British fighter support, and that the planes would be needed to defend Britain. He said "no." In other words, he decided that it would be a low-leverage action. He was proved right when Hitler began his air attack on Britain. Without the planes, Britain wouldn't have withstood Hitler's massive bombing attack.

A second, difficult, leverage-point decision was necessary when France surrendered to Germany. Churchill did not want the French Navy to fall into German hands, so he asked the French admiral to either join the British Navy or demobilize his ships. When the admiral refused, the British Navy seized all French ships in British waters and sank or disabled all the other French ships it could find. Churchill recognized this as a high-leverage point because the Germans would reap a large benefit from the French ships, and only a small amount of British resources was required to seize or sink them.

Leverage Points of Expertise

John Browne, the CEO of BP (formerly British Petroleum), insists that "everyone in the company who is not directly accountable for a profit be involved in creating and distributing knowledge that the company can use to make a profit." He says, "The key to reaping a big return is to leverage knowledge by sharing it throughout the company so each unit is not learning in isolation."

To expand on Browne's idea, consider expertise as a valuable resource. Then consider that, when learning takes place in one part of an organization, a great deal of the investment to learn already has been made. A leverage point of expertise is any place in an organization where known expertise can be applied to get large benefits.

Leverage Points in Time

It is common practice to shorten the time it takes to finish a project by having planners find the path in the project that takes the longest time and then work to reduce the time on that path (often called critical path planning). These critical paths that are projected to hold up the entire project should be treated like the time when the chest cavity is open during open-heart surgery and blood is being bypassed around the heart—that is, holdups should be minimized as much as possible. You may ask what would be an acceptable reason to interrupt the surgeon during this time: taking a nonemergency call from his daughter or his stockbroker, or from a racquetball buddy who wants to arrange a match?

When a major portion of the project is held up until an action is finished, we should use the rules for the surgeon when the chest cavity is open.

Edison, Gates, and Smith worked all night with the person at the high-leverage point. When Curie knew she was onto something, she worked nonstop. Of course, any good concept can be carried too far. However, in this fast-paced world, we teach the open-heart-surgery principle and many other models and concepts to companies that want to reduce product development time and time to market.

Leverage Points in Battle

In 1940, the freedom of the world was threatened as Hitler rolled his war machine across Europe. He seemed unstoppable. On December 7, 1943, U.S. president Franklin Delano Roosevelt flew to Tunis, where he was whisked from his plane and placed in General Dwight D. Eisenhower's car. As the car drove off, he turned to Eisenhower and said, "Ike, you're going to command Overlord." Operation Overlord was the code name for the Invasion of Normandy—history's greatest sea-to-land battle.

Throughout his life, Eisenhower was chosen to lead important missions. Why? Because he had a high batting average of successful missions. He was not only well-prepared for opportunity; he almost always delivered great returns to investors in the mission. He delivered because his thinking was both high leverage and high meaning.

His high-leverage thinking can be seen in the way in which the invasion was planned. He knew that attacks from sea to land are inherently difficult and generally unsuccessful. Although he had commanded successful, large-scale sea-to-land operations in North Africa, Sicily, and Salerno, these were not direct frontal attacks from the sea against highly fortified land positions. So he knew he had to find high-leverage points.

The Germans had constructed a seemingly impenetrable wall of fortified gun bunkers along the French coast. The shores were heavily mined. On the other side of the wall were 20 divisions of battle-hardened, heavily armed, highly mobile Panzers under the command of the legendary Field Marshall Erwin Rommel. The Germans could launch a massive counterattack with over 100,000 troops within days of the first attack. Behind all that were 600,000 heavily armed German troops, allocated to defend France.

Eisenhower knew that, to win over superior forces, he had to concentrate his forces, act with speed, be mobile, and surprise the enemy. Because the Germans had to defend over 3,500 miles of coastline, running from Holland to the southern end of the Bay of Biscay, they had to spread out their forces. In contrast, the Allies could concentrate their forces on a small part of the coastline and surprise the Germans. The Allies chose five beaches on the Normandy coast as high-leverage points (figure 9-3).

Because most high-leverage points exist only in narrow windows of time, they must be seized quickly. Eisenhower knew that the invading troops would be outnumbered six to one if Rommel were able to move his full force toward Normandy. Eisenhower decided to decrease the mobility and speed of Rommel's divisions by bombing all the railroads and bridges behind Rommel's forces. This would isolate them from their supply lines. Ike also decided that the Allies would bomb Rommel's tanks if he moved them forward. These were high-leverage-point bombings:

> SINCE THE FOCUS OF EFFORT REPRESENTS OUR BID FOR VICTORY, WE MUST DIRECT IT AT THAT OBJECT WHICH WILL CAUSE THE MOST DECISIVE DAMAGE TO THE ENEMY AND WHICH HOLDS THE BEST OPPORTUNITY OF SUCCESS. . . . IT FORCES US TO CONCENTRATE DECISIVE COMBAT POWER JUST AS IT FORCES US TO ACCEPT RISK. THUS, WE FOCUS OUR EFFORT AGAINST CRITICAL ENEMY VULNERABILITY, EXERCISING STRICT ECONOMY ELSEWHERE. (FROM *WARFIGHTING: THE U.S. MARINE CORPS BOOK OF STRATEGY*)

Figure 9-3. American soldiers landing at Omaha Beach for
Operation Overlord during World War II (© Corbis)

However, the air forces were not under Eisenhower's command. The generals who headed the air forces believed that strategic bombing of German industry and terror bombing of German cities would end the war, and that Operation Overlord was not necessary. Eisenhower believed that these views were dangerous nonsense—that a fanatical, resolved Hitler would fight to the death and would have to be defeated on the ground. Hitler proved Eisenhower right.

Convinced that bombing before and during the invasion was essential and high leverage, Eisenhower gambled his career on it. In London, he told the combined chiefs of staff, "Every obstacle must be overcome, every inconvenience suffered, and every risk run to ensure that our blow is decisive. We cannot afford to fail." He threatened to step down from the position of commander-in-chief if he weren't given the support of the air commands. He got his air support, and later it would be clear to everyone, including the objecting air commanders, that he was right. He had seen what others hadn't seen and was willing to stake his career on it.

How Do We Act at Multiple Points in an Organized Campaign?

When the great achievers found high-leverage points, they organized teams and designed action plans to act on all the points available, in a timely, coordinated way. Eisenhower and his staff divided the overall mission into smaller, coordinated missions that were focused on high-leverage points. The records of his battles include an example of the overall Overlord mission and a small, coordinated mission at a high-leverage point:

MISSION OF ENTIRE ALLIED EXPEDITIONARY FORCE BEFORE THE INVASION OF NORMANDY: YOU WILL ENTER THE CONTINENT OF EUROPE AND, IN CONJUNCTION WITH THE OTHER UNITED NATIONS, UNDERTAKE OPERATIONS AIMED AT THE HEART OF GERMANY AND THE DESTRUCTION OF HER ARMED FORCES. AFTER ADEQUATE CHANNEL PORTS HAVE BEEN SECURED, SECURE AN AREA THAT WILL FACILITATE BOTH GROUND AND AIR OPERATIONS AGAINST THE ENEMY.

HIGH-LEVERAGE-POINT MISSION ASSIGNED TO ENGLAND'S SIXTH AIRBORNE DIVISION OF PARATROOPERS DURING THE INVASION: LAND ON THE EASTERN END OF THE BEACHHEAD NEAR CAEN. ONCE THERE, CARRY OUT THE FOLLOWING TASKS: SECURE CROSSINGS OVER THE ORNE RIVER AND CAEN CANAL, KNOCK OUT BIG COASTAL GUNS IN THE AREA, AND BLOCK GERMAN REINFORCEMENTS FROM REACH-ING THE ALLIED TROOPS LANDING ON THE BEACHES.

All the high-leverage points were acted on in a well-timed, well-executed invasion. In the early hours of the invasion, Special Forces were dropped behind the enemy's lines to direct massive naval guns that would pound the German fortifications just before the first troops landed. Commando teams were dropped in by gliders and by parachute to blow up key bridges and secure important positions. Thousands of individual missions at high-leverage points were planned and timed to support the main thrust, the landing at five beaches on the Normandy coast.

Acting at many high-leverage points in an organized, timely way increases the probability that you will achieve large returns, even if action at one of the high-leverage points fails or if you have high, unexpected losses, such as those the American forces suffered at Omaha Beach, a code name for one of the beaches. Figure 9-4 shows how this increases your chances of success.

There are possibilities that you could become blocked at a critical leverage point. You should have backup plans for the critical points. Risk is reduced by planning well, by assessing risks at critical points, by taking preemptive action if possible, and by focusing at high-leverage points. When you put small amounts of resources at multiple high-leverage points, you minimize losses if one doesn't pay off.

High-Meaning Thinking at High-Leverage Points

From his past combat leadership, Eisenhower knew that the success of the invasion of Normandy depended heavily on the front wave of soldiers. If the soldiers came

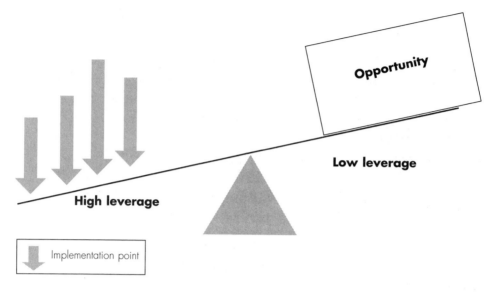

Figure 9-4. Organized implementation at multiple points improves the success rate.

storming out of the landing crafts and attacked the enemy, the invasion would succeed. If they cowered behind the landing crafts, the invasion would fail.

So Eisenhower spent his evenings and weekends with soldiers that were part of the first assaults. He said that every soldier who risks his life should know why, and he should see, face to face, the man who was leading him into battle.

In the four months before D-Day, Ike visited 26 divisions, 24 airfields, 5 ships, and countless depots, shops, and hospitals. He gave a short speech at each site about defending the future freedom of all people. He said that the men were fighting for their loved ones back home and for the lives they would return to when the war was over. Then he made the rounds, shaking hands and asking questions (figure 9-5).

Whereas other generals asked the men about their military specialties, training, units, or weapons, Eisenhower asked them, "Where are you from?" "What did you do back home?" "What are your plans for when the war is over?" "Who's waiting back home for you?" To other generals, these were soldiers. To Eisenhower, they were citizen-soldiers, caught up in a war that none of them wanted. He knew that what meant the most to them were those they had left behind.

Stories of his inspiring conversations with the men quickly spread through the camps after he left. The troops knew that Eisenhower saw the war through their eyes and knew what really had meaning for them. The soldiers in the Normandy inva-

Figure 9-5. The Supreme Allied commander, General Dwight D. Eisenhower, talking with paratroopers before D-Day (© Corbis)

sion fought valiantly. The invasion was so successful that Soviet premier Joseph Stalin, who seldom praised anyone or anything, said, "The history of war does not know of an undertaking comparable to it for breadth of conception, grandeur of scale, and mastery of execution."

Questions on High-Leverage Planning and Last Thoughts

To ensure that you have a high-leverage action plan to seize an opportunity, you may ask yourself these kinds of questions:

- Is the plan organized in high-leverage thrusts? Does each thrust have the optimum resources?
- Are the critical high-leverage points identified along with their risks? Have backup or contingency plans been developed?
- Do we have the resources to carry it out? Have we planned and committed resources at the high-leverage points?
- Is there a detailed plan that specifies actions, resource applications, timing, assignment of responsibilities, and measures of success? Has each person with a stake in the opportunity accepted responsibility for his or her assigned actions?
- Are events scheduled to minimize total implementation time and total resource consumption, while maximizing the final outcome?

One last thought on seizing opportunity: If a great opportunity or threat exists, it's only a matter of time before other great achievers will find it and seize it. If we don't prepare for, find, and seize the great opportunities that come our way, we suffer the costs of lost opportunities and the loss of potential return on our time, ideas, energy, and resources.

 Self-Evaluation Exercise

List opportunities from earlier exercises and/or identify opportunities from other areas of your life. Place these in the left-hand column below. Then, for each opportunity, list critical high-leverage points for implementation in the right-hand column.

Opportunity	Critical High-Leverage Points
Create new drive-through coffee business	Understand business model of competitor; explore partnering opportunities; attend retail franchising conference; test market ideas in low-overhead location

Example

Develop Leaders

It has been proven time and time again that the only leader whom soldiers will reliably follow when their lives are on the line is the leader who is both competent and whom soldiers believe is committed to their well-being.

—Peter Senge, *The Fifth Discipline*

Finally, key 10 is to lead investors to seize the opportunity and the rewards. This sets great leaders apart. They know the answer to these questions:

- Why are some leaders chosen to lead over and over again?
- How do we ensure that shareholders will invest again?

Why Are Some Leaders Chosen to Lead Again and Again?

Great leaders are chosen to lead again because they deliver rewards to stakeholders. There was no one more determined to deliver rewards to investors than General Dwight D. Eisenhower. He had to deliver to the U.S. Congress, the Joint Chiefs of Staff, his field commanders, his troops, Roosevelt, Churchill, Stalin, and the people in the Allied countries. His desire to deliver stood out when Walter Cronkite interviewed him 20 years after the invasion of Normandy. Eisenhower said little about battles, commanders, politicians, or strategies. Instead, he spoke of the men and women who died in the war, who never enjoyed their grandchildren—whom he didn't deliver for.

When World War II ended, Eisenhower returned to the United States as a hero. When he spoke to a joint session of Congress, he received the longest standing ovation in congressional history. He was persuaded to enter politics and went on to serve two terms as president of the United States. He was chosen to lead time and time again because he led investors to seize great opportunities, and he made sure that the benefits of opportunities were delivered to investors.

Great leaders deliver even when times are tough. In 1986, when FedEx shut down its Zapmail program, it found other jobs in the company for those affected. When it discontinued some operations in Europe, it placed full-page ads urging other employers to hire its workers. In Belgium, 80 companies responded with 600 job offers. Loyalty in hard times builds a "trust fund" that pays long-term dividends. FedEx founder Fred Smith believes that if you take care of your people, they will take care of your customers, the company will be profitable, and your people will have secure futures. For more on the FedEx story, see *The 100 Best Companies to Work for in America* by Robert Levering, Milton Moskowitz, and Michael Katz (New York: New American Library, 1987).

For years, companies like IBM, AT&T, and GE rewarded loyal employees by assuring them lifetime job security. But when business went bad and Wall Street rewarded companies that made job cuts, the companies laid off people—an example of failure to deliver.

We, the authors, have worked with a corporation in Chicago that has delivered to employees by never having a layoff in its 65-year history. Its employees are willing to create improvements because they know they won't lose their jobs as a result. They have improved manufacturing labor productivity every year and have increased the customer delivery response rate by 10 to 1. The CEO of the company feels responsible for delivering to the people he leads.

How Do We Ensure That Shareholders Will Invest Again?

The key to ensuring that shareholders will invest again is to deliver what means the most to them. Great leaders deliver. In 1981, the government of France awarded Louis Pasteur a medal for developing the vaccines and the antiseptic concepts discussed earlier in the book. But Pasteur said he would refuse the medal unless the government also gave awards to his research assistants. Many chose to be led by Pasteur because he delivered the benefits.

Bill Gates has delivered to the employees who helped him to build Microsoft. He's created more employee millionaires than anyone else in history.

Successful leaders respect the expertise and resources of stakeholders and feel responsible for seeing that their investment is rewarded. Stakeholders judge leaders by what they deliver, not what they promise. If they don't deliver, the stakeholders may not willingly invest again. Stakeholders seem to know the old saying: I can't hear what you're saying because what you are doing is so loud! (Ralph Waldo Emerson may be the first to have said this.)

Personal Success Versus Organizational Success

When it comes to delivering, the noted researcher Jim Collins says in his book *Good to Great* (New York: Harper Collins, 2001) that the most successful executives put the organization's success ahead of their own. He says that they go beyond effective leadership. They build the organization's enduring greatness through a mix of humility and professional will.

We all are inclined to put our personal successes first, rather than the contributions we can make to others. However, people such as Edison, Smith, Einstein, Curie, Walton, and Michelangelo achieved personal success as a result of the important contributions they made to others. In free societies, those who have delivered great benefits to stakeholders have been more successful personally.

If stakeholders believe that they have received good value for their investments, they'll invest again in opportunities the leader helps them find—and the leader will be chosen to lead again. These investments can be in a wide variety of benefits, such as

- personal growth
- security
- the opportunity to create
- social recognition
- financial success
- a better society
- food for the soul.

Great innovators and achievers not only deliver; they also develop others so that they can also find and seize the great opportunities of their time. Developing other innovators and high achievers is the highest level of leadership, and many can't reach it. Let's look at an example of a brilliant, hard-working, ambitious man who failed because he fell short of this level.

William Shockley Fails to Coach Others to Lead

In 1945, radios, telephone circuits, and transmitters built with vacuum tubes were heavy, bulky, expensive, and unreliable, and they required a lot of power to operate. So Bell Labs, the research division of AT&T, formed a scientific team to find a replacement for the vacuum tube and appointed William Shockley to lead it.

Shockley knew that the person who invented a replacement device would lead a revolution in electronics, computers, and communication systems. He had an idea, and, for a year and a half, two scientists on his team, John Bardeen and Walter Brattain, tried to make his idea work. Bardeen created hundreds of designs, and Brattain built them and tested them. They all failed. From the failures, Bardeen developed a theory that led the team in another direction.

Following Bardeen's theory, in late December 1947, Brattain positioned a tiny, V-shaped probe against the surface of a small piece of germanium. He saw an unexpected signal on the screen of his oscilloscope. He blurted out, "This thing's got gain," for everyone in the quiet laboratory to hear. After Bardeen quickly made some calculations, the team members knew they had found a new phenomenon. Their activity increased to a feverish pace. Within a month, they had a working device that eventually was called a transistor.

Shockley was furious when they told him that they had discovered how to replace the vacuum tube in a way entirely different from what he had proposed. Also, because he was at home when they made the discovery, he was afraid that he might not get all the credit. He immediately went into seclusion and worked around the clock to create an advanced version of the transistor that would upstage what they had discovered.

When photos of the moment of the breakthrough were staged for the press, Shockley grabbed the seat that Brattain had been in when the discovery was made, creating the impression that he had made the discovery. At a press conference, Shockley also gave the false impression that Brattain had simply been following his instructions. He tried in vain to convince patent attorneys that his name should be the only name on the patent. Although the Nobel Prize for the transistor was awarded to all three men, Bardeen and Brattain were deeply troubled by Shockley's attempt to take all the credit.

Shockley later started his own company, and he tried to hire scientists from AT&T. Each one turned him down, so he hired scientists who didn't know him well. Within his company, Shockley was so controlling over the work of the scientists that they could not pursue their own ideas. Scientists with leadership ability became frustrated.

They found other opportunities and left to create Fairchild Semiconductors and Intel. Shockley's company failed.

Many leaders have known how to find great opportunity and seize it. Many of them also have been able to attract investors and deliver benefits. But, like Shockley, some of them never enabled others to develop into innovators or high achievers or leaders of innovators and high achievers. Such leaders believe that only they can achieve at a high level and that they lose something when others succeed. They may fear that they will lose power, followers, control, or the chance to achieve again.

So the questions are:

- Why should we enable others to develop?
- How should we enable others to develop?

Compare Shockley with Sam Walton. Walton was an innovator and a high achiever who developed others for their benefit and for the benefit of his organization. Early in the development of Wal-Mart, he realized that one of the great pitfalls of expanding a business was in not developing strong leader-managers. He also knew how much retail management expertise it took to become a strong leader-manager. So he went after leaders. In his words, "Without shame or embarrassment, I nosed around other people's stores searching for talent."

Walton was nosing around a successful TG&Y store in Tulsa when he ran into the store manager, Willard Walker. Walton was so impressed with Walker that he offered him a salary and a percentage of the profits to manage Walton's first expansion store. A percentage of the profits was Walton's way of delivering to those who helped him build Wal-Mart. He knew that complex organizations can't be grown without people who have expertise in leading and developing other innovators and high achievers. He believed that, if developed, others could achieve as much as he could. Later, he developed managers from within the company to manage new stores as they opened.

Developing others is an important leadership responsibility. The next leader, Phil Jackson, is a master of both. He has helped some of basketball's best players become leaders of high achievers.

The "Jordan Problem"

By 1989, Michael Jordan of the Chicago Bulls was the best basketball player and the leading scorer in the National Basketball Association (NBA). Because he could take control of a game at will, competitors feared him, and his teammates were in awe of him. But the Bulls' head coach, Doug Collins, and his staff regularly discussed what they called the "Jordan problem." Because Jordan was the Bulls' major scoring threat, other teams beat them by double teaming him. Teammates keyed their play around him and were reluctant to initiate plays independently.

The Bulls attempted many solutions. In one staff meeting, assistant coach Phil Jackson said that he believed the mark of a great player was not how much he scored but how much he lifted his teammate's performances. Collins told Jackson to tell that to Jordan. Reluctantly, Jackson approached Jordan in the weight-training room and told him Holzman's point of view. Jordan thanked him for the advice.

The following season, Jordan agreed to become a point guard, direct the offense, and bring other players into the key. It seemed to work, at first. But, by the time the Bulls lost in the Eastern Conference finals, it was clear that, after running as point guard and directing the offense, Jordan didn't have the energy left for the last quarter drive.

When Jackson replaced Collins as head coach of the Bulls, he searched for an opportunity to lift the whole team to a championship level. He decided that he needed to replace its traditional power offense.

Jackson felt that a power offense was creative in the hands of a great player like Jordan, but it involved only two or three players in any given play. He needed an offense that involved all the players in a play. He decided to change to a triangle offense designed by assistant coach Tex Winters.

Jackson had to persuade Jordan to try the triangle offense and to lead the team in a way that helped the other players to become high achievers and come together as a team. He had to replace the meaning Jordan would lose as the team star. He had to sell Jordan the idea that helping his teammates to be all they could be was the key to an NBA title.

In his book, *Sacred Hoops* (New York: Hyperion, 1995), Jackson recalls asking Jordan to help him lead the switch to a new triangle offense and to share the spotlight with his teammates to help them grow into high achievers:

> JORDAN: WELL, I THINK WE'RE GOING TO HAVE TROUBLE WHEN THE BALL GETS TO CERTAIN PEOPLE, BECAUSE THEY CAN'T PASS AND THEY CAN'T MAKE DECISIONS WITH THE BALL.

> JACKSON: I UNDERSTAND THAT. BUT I THINK IF YOU GIVE THE SYSTEM A CHANCE, THEY'LL LEARN TO BE PLAYMAKERS. THE IMPORTANT THING IS TO LET EVERYBODY TOUCH THE BALL, SO THEY WON'T FEEL LIKE SPECTATORS. YOU CAN'T BEAT A GOOD DEFENSIVE TEAM WITH ONE MAN. IT'S GOT TO BE A TEAM EFFORT.

> JORDAN: OKAY, YOU KNOW ME. I'VE ALWAYS BEEN A COACHABLE PLAYER. WHATEVER YOU WANT TO DO, I'M BEHIND YOU.

From that time on, Jordan devoted himself to making the new system work, and Jackson devoted himself to persuading each player to surrender his "me" for the "we" of being part of a team with a great mission. Beginning in 1991, the Bulls jelled as a team and won three straight NBA titles.

Today, Jackson has nine NBA titles—as many as anyone in NBA history. He elevates the players and the team above himself. Although some argue that his teams won just because they had great players, Shaquille O'Neal knows better. After Jackson left the Bulls, he moved to Los Angeles and led the Lakers, starring O'Neal, to three straight NBA titles. O'Neal said he would have no title rings if it were not for Jackson.

O'Neal and Jordan played a combined 13 seasons and never won a championship without Phil Jackson as coach.

Innovators and High Achievers Are Made, Not Born

For centuries, people debated why some individuals achieve greatness—whether it was God-given ability, the right early environment, perseverance, courage, hard work, or luck. Alexander the Great and Napoleon Bonaparte, who were larger-than-life military leaders, often are cited as examples of great leaders who were born to lead. Alexander was the son of a king and a princess, and Aristotle taught him. Napoleon's father was a lawyer, and Napoleon was educated at the prestigious Brienne and the École Militaire.

However, for every Alexander or Napoleon, history provides examples of people born to power and privilege who were low achievers and poor leaders. For example, Louis XVI was the grandson of a king, and his wife, Marie Antionette, was the daughter of an emperor and an empress. Louis was weak and incapable and preferred to spend his time playing instead of leading. While the country was in financial crises, Marie flaunted her wealth. When hungry mobs marched on the palace, she refused to make any concessions and set the troops on them. At a time of great crises, both of them failed.

We don't believe that innovators, high achievers, or great leaders are born with all the skills to succeed. Yet even if they are, they still must develop their talents. Great leaders know that people and organizations must be taught to take powerful keys to reach their potential.

By the time World War II broke out, Eisenhower and Churchill were already near the top of their respective fields. Most great leaders—such as Fred Smith, Oprah Winfrey, Dwight Eisenhower, Sam Walton, Winston Churchill, and Abraham Lincoln—rose from the bottom to the top of their fields. They knew that leaders are made and that leadership could be taught.

With the keys for finding great opportunities, we maximize the chances that we'll find the great opportunities of our time. With the keys to mobilize support, we can find the highest meanings of others and motivate them to invest their time, ideas, and resources. With the keys to seize great opportunities, we can rapidly seize the opportunities and deliver the rewards. Great innovative leadership is the result of mastering these 10 keys.

To close this book, let's return to this profound ability of the most successful people.

The Profound Aspect of the Keys

More than 500 years ago, the powerful and rich Lorenzo de' Medici brought Michelangelo to live in his palace after he discovered Michelangelo's talent. Lorenzo also brought many of the fine poets, writers, and philosophers of the times to live in his palace.

Many of these gifted people were followers of the ancient Greek philosopher Plato. Plato believed that people, buildings, and mountains are imperfect copies of ideal forms that exist in the ideal realm. He said that our souls come from the ideal realm and that we can remember these ideal forms if we search deeply for them. Young Michelangelo absorbed these ideas and combined them with his Christian beliefs. He came to believe that the ideal form was an idea held in the mind of God, and it was his creative task to see it and to free it from its marble bonds.

That is why Michelangelo saw David staring at Goliath, the enemy, at the moment of decision, not at the moment of triumph—as other artists had. That is why he was able to see where David was in the stone before he began to carve.

In closing, we hope that these 10 keys will inspire you to become more than you are today. We also hope that following the path of these great leaders will move you closer to capturing the profound ability to find and seize opportunities that lead to great success.

Self-Evaluation Exercise

Pertaining to your own leadership skills, you . . .

✓	
	Put your organization's success above your own
	Develop others to grow and contribute
	Take interest in finding and delivering that which is most meaningful to stakeholders
	Coach others to be successful
	Search for others' skills and special abilities, then help them find areas where they can maximize their effectiveness
	Believe that your personal success is tied to helping others to maximize their effectiveness

Place a check in the left-hand column for all that apply.

About the Authors

 **Greg Swartz** is director of business technology development for PING Inc. leading new product introductions and innovations. Before joining PING, he was director of manufacturing for Conn-Selmer and director of consulting for Competitive Action Inc. He has led or facilitated the successful redesign of more than 20 business and manufacturing systems and has developed multiple lean enterprise training initiatives. He holds a bachelor's degree in electrical engineering from the University of Evansville, Evansville, Indiana.

 **Julie K. Thorpe** is the president of Competitive Action, Inc., a consulting and training firm. She has more than 20 years of business and technical experience. She has held management positions at GTE and Cygnus Systems, Inc., and received her bachelor's degree in computer science from Indiana State University.

James B. Swartz has 26 years of industry experience and has helped hundreds of organizations find great opportunities. He is the author of The Hunters and the Hunted, a widely acclaimed book on nonlinear process improvements for the workplace. He is a sought-after speaker, consultant, and workshop leader. He has an MS in Physics as a Bardeen Scholar from the University of Illinois.

Joseph E. Swartz is director of business transformation at St. Francis Hospital and Health Centers of Indianapolis, Indiana. He has facilitated improvement projects in large companies such as Eli Lilly, General Motors, and Honeywell as well as in numerous smaller companies. Swartz holds an MS in management from Purdue University, where he graduated as a Krannert Scholar.

Laura J. Louis has 13 years of manufacturing experience as an industrial engineer, business analyst, and project management professional with Micron Technology, Inc. She holds a BSEE and earned her MS in operations management from Purdue University, Krannert School of Management. Prior experience includes manufacturing consulting with Competitive Action, Inc. and manufacturing engineering for Delco Electronics.

Index